The **4 ESSENTIALS**

A Misfit's Journey to
Mindset, Strategies, Values & Purpose

With Over 100 Famous Mentors and Entrepreneurs

Cliff Michaels

About The Author

Cliff Michaels has been a broker, strategic coach, angel investor, education activist, and social entrepreneur for over 25 years. His online programs and live training provide *Essentials* for life, careers, teachers, and entrepreneurs. From 1996-2004, Cliff was a member, education chair, forum trainer, and President of the Young Entrepreneurs' Organization Los Angeles Chapter (known today as EO). He launched EO's first student mentor programs and philanthropy events. Cliff Michaels & Associates (real estate, mortgages, investments) has closed one billion dollars in transactions since 1992. Cliff was also Co-Founder of First Use (1999), a pioneering online platform that featured the world's first digital-notary technology. A Southern California native, Cliff's passions include movies, music, yoga, animal rights, helping kids at risk, and raising the bar for global education.

About The Book
(available in audio, e-book, paperback)

In 2012, *The 4 Essentials* launched #1 on Amazon and #3 on the New York Times Bestseller List. Taking readers on a street-smart journey through life, mentors, and business, Cliff proposes a radical shift in global education and career training. He also provides thought-provoking stories on *The 4 Essentials* (*mindset, strategies, values, purpose*) which dispel myths on how we define and create success. Through trials and triumphs, Cliff shares lessons from the edge as a dyslexic student who challenged the status quo in college, dropped out of USC at 19, and launched companies in real estate, finance, education, and technology (all before age 30). Drawing on over 100 famous mentors from Socrates, Edison, and da Vinci to Oprah, Malala, Branson, and Mycoskie, Cliff empowers each of us to earn a real-world MBA (Master's in Basic Abilities). This is a fun, fast-paced read for anyone in search of passion, purpose, and results!

To sponsor a club or school with books & e-courses, visit CliffMichaels.com

Cliff Michaels Learning

A path to profits, passion, and purpose
with dynamic e-courses, forums & retreats

Step 1 · Career & Personal Growth

Self & Team Discovery
Personal & Professional Essentials

Career Builder
Resumes, Interviews, Networking

Communication & Relationships
Social & Business Intelligence

Goal, Project & Time Management
Better Work Flow to Get Things Done

Money Master & Steps to 800 Credit
A Guide to Financial Freedom

The Achiever's Mindset
A Path to Unlimited Success

Step 2 · The Entrepreneur's Edge

The Brainstormer
Secrets to Hack Ideas

Lead, Manage & Motivate
Team Building & Culture Fit

The Power Negotiator
Keys to Closing & Conflict Resolution

The Entrepreneur's Pitch & Plan
Angels, Demons & Start-Up Strategies

Sales · Marketing · Branding
A Power Play to Profits

Forum Training & Facilitating
Effective Teams, Boards & Meetings

Essentials for Life, Careers & Entrepreneurs

Learn More at CliffMichaels.com

Praise

"Cliff's writing is full of creativity, inspiration, and practical lessons. Highly recommend for students and professionals!"

BLAKE MYCOSKIE

Founder, Chief Shoe Giver, TOMS Shoes, NY Times Bestseller (*Start Something That Matters*)

"Cliff Michaels delivers a powerful path to profits, passion, and purpose!"

TONY HSIEH

CEO, Zappos.com, NY Times Bestseller (*Delivering Happiness*)

"The 4 Essentials is a fun read! Like Cliff, it's full of passion with a blend of new ideas and timeless wisdom."

DAVE LOGAN

Former Assoc. Dean, USC Marshall Business School, NY Times Bestseller (*Tribal Leadership*)

"There's too much theory out there. Cliff provides a real-world framework for success. Thanks for bringing this important resource to the world."

DOUG MELLINGER

Managing Director of Clarion Capital

"Cliff Michaels provides entrepreneurial conditioning with an achiever's mindset."

DARREN HARDY

Publisher of SUCCESS Magazine

*"Cliff's concept for a **Master's in Basic Abilities** hits the nail on the head. He takes us on a life journey with pragmatic insights for anyone on their entrepreneurial path."*

SUE HESSE

Director of Foundation Partnerships, Kauffman Foundation

The 4 Essentials
A Misfit's Journey to Mindset, Strategies, Values & Purpose
© Copyright 2016 • All rights reserved
2016 2nd Edition: ISBN 978-0-9975243-1-4
Published by Cliff Michaels & Associates, Inc.
PO 6156, Thousand Oaks, CA 91359

Previously titled: **The 4 Essentials of Entrepreneurial Thinking**
What Successful People Didn't Learn in School
© Copyright 2012 • All rights reserved
Cliff Michaels & Associates, Inc.
2012 First Edition: ISBN 13: 978-0-615-45055-1

For speaking, interviews, workshops, forums, private retreats, or bulk orders, please visit: **www.cliffmichaels.com**

Neither the author nor publisher provides legal or financial advice with this book. The reader is advised to seek their own professionals for legal and financial services.

Printed in the United States of America

Mission

Inspire, give back, and raise the bar
for global education and entrepreneurship

Global Giving

We donate books and e-courses
to students, clubs, and schools each day

CliffMichaels.Com

E-learning, group forums, and global retreats
for life, careers, and entrepreneurs

Dedication

To the misfits, rebels, and crazy ones
who make a positive change in the world

To friends, family, and clients,
who made this book an amazing journey

To Inspirational Mentors in This Book

"In my walks, every person I meet
is my superior in some way, and in that, I learn from them."
RALPH WALDO EMERSON

Jessica Alba • Buddha • Muhammad Ali • Maya Angelou • Michelangelo • Aristotle Lucille Ball • Jeff Bezos • Sara Blakely • Richard Branson • Matthew Broderick Herb Brooks • Warren Buffett • Lewis Carroll • Charles Darwin • Leonardo da Vinci • Ellen DeGeneres • Charles Dickens • Peter Drucker • Thomas Edison Albert Einstein • Ralph Waldo Emerson • Anne Frank • Benjamin Franklin Mohatma Gandhi • Howard Gardner • Bill Gates • Kahlil Gibran • Malcolm Gladwell • Wayne Gretzky • Seth Godin • Daniel Goleman • Napoleon Hill Tony Hsieh • John Hughes • Helen Keller • Dave Logan • Elisabeth Kubler-Ross Steve Jobs • Magic Johnson • Michael Jordan • Dalai Lama • Bruce Lee • John Lennon • Abraham Lincoln • Jennifer Lopez • Martin Luther King, Jr. • Nelson Mandela • Vinnie Marino • Mary Mazzio • Mozart • Blake Mycoskie • Pelé Laurence Peter • Pablo Picasso • Queen Latifah • Daniel Radcliffe • Ken Robinson Knute Rockne • J.K. Rowling • Babe Ruth • J.D. Salinger • Howard Schultz Will Smith • Socrates • Steven Spielberg • Oliver Stone • J.R.R. Tolkien • Mark Twain • Oscar Wilde • Oprah Winfrey • John Wooden • Tiger Woods • Malala Yousafzai • Robin Williams • Venus & Serena Williams

... and Lucy The Warrior Pup

How This Book is Structured

1) In the introduction, I'll explain why I wrote this book, and then propose a simple strategy to raise the bar for global education and entrepreneurship.

2) In a mini-memoir, I'll share *My Lessons From the Edge* — a misfit's journey over 30 years through life, school, and business.

3) In *The 4 Essentials*, I'll provide dozens of stories on *Mindset*, *Strategies*, *Values*, and *Purpose* that I learned from many mentors. Together, we'll discover a dynamic system for success and happiness!

Cliff Michaels

> *"There is something inherently valuable about being a misfit. It's not to say that every person who has artistic talent is a social outcast, but there is definitely value in identifying yourself differently, and being proud of it."*
>
> DANIEL RADCLIFFE (HARRY POTTER)
> Actor (Misfit Wizard)

Table of Contents

Introduction

The Misfits, Rebels & Troublemakers

IN 1997, STEVE JOBS ran a famous TV commercial for Apple Computers, featuring seventeen iconic misfits, from Einstein and Earhart to Ali and Gandhi. They were the crazy ones who taught us to think different, put square pegs in round holes, challenge the status quo, and change the world.

Growing up, I always felt like a misfit, especially in school and social circles. I'm dyslexic so I struggled with math and reading. As a home-alone kid of divorced parents, I had no traditional mentors and went through nine schools before turning 16. Despite a somewhat challenging childhood, I was accepted to USC. I dropped out after one year, but had a college experience that forever changed my outlook on life, business, and education — I was fascinated by what successful people *didn't* learn in school.

As college freshmen in 1985, classmates and I had the audacity to ask why we had to take prerequisite courses that had nothing to do with our talent or career goals. Did every aspiring artist or athlete need to be proficient in advanced math or science? Did every doctor or engineer need to excel in art or foreign languages? Many courses felt no more relevant than those we took in high school (tuition was far more expensive though).

At the time, I had an internship with real estate mentors who taught me a few *Essentials* such as budgets, negotiation, time management, creative thinking, social skills, and the power of thank-you notes. These lessons were conspicuously absent from most school programs, so I proposed a theory to professors that I felt could fill a gap for students and professionals — a real-world MBA (Master's in Basic Abilities). My research not only rocked the boat at USC, but served as my passport to a unique adventure through life and business.

Ambitious but broke, I left college early to find the missing link between what traditional education teaches and *The 4 Essentials* critical to success. As I take you on a journey through inspirational mentors, you'll learn why I admired innovators like Thomas Edison, social entrepreneurs like Blake Mycoskie, and creative writers like J.K. Rowling. I also studied artists, athletes, and peacemakers to see what they could teach us about passion, purpose, profits, and pitfalls.

If you come along, I promise a more rewarding trip than you ever imagined ...

i

An Education Revolution from Classrooms to Careers

My research for this book is based on 25 years of experience as a student, entrepreneur, and education activist. I've consulted teachers and leaders around the globe about what works and doesn't in classrooms and career training. To that end, I'm a part-time philosopher and full-time truth seeker.

THE KEY QUESTION: Is success assured if an individual has talent, nurturing, job opportunities, and access to the best schools? The undeniable answer is "No." There are millions of gifted, privileged, well-educated people who fail miserably in life. On the flipside, there are highly-accomplished people who transcend poverty, adversity, physical challenges, and education gaps. Muhammad Ali, Oprah Winfrey, and Abraham Lincoln came from humble beginnings and broke new ground for generations to follow. Innovators like Lucille Ball, Richard Branson, and Helen Keller had learning challenges, but still raised the bar in their fields. Teenager Malala Yousafzai was shot by a terrorist, and activist Nelson Mandela was unjustly imprisoned for 27 years, yet they both went on to win The Nobel Peace Prize. What can we conclude from all these *so-called misfits?*

The notion that an individual's potential is predicated solely on academic, financial, physical, or social advantage is categorically false.

Bridging Gaps Between Old & New School

Seemingly challenged people prove every day that achievement is the result of learning highly-connected *Essentials* that equate to a real-world MBA (**M**aster's in **B**asic **A**bilities). Moreover, if we measure success by health, happiness, and contribution to society, we discover the need for a larger set of *Essentials* than any of us are born with. With that in mind, why wouldn't we teach a more holistic system for life and career results in every classroom and workplace?

Old habits and bureaucracy are no longer excuses. We can easily drive change by first acknowledging our unique abilities (visual, verbal, social, left brain, right brain). Some of us need to sing and dance, while others need structure and spreadsheets. Since learning programs should be as diverse as students, the days of static, top-down, standardized education are as useful as a square wheel.

OLD SCHOOL		NEW SCHOOL
Top Down	vs.	Bottom Up
Teacher Centric	vs.	Student-Driven
Passive & Isolated	vs.	Active, Peer-to-Peer Collaboration
Memorized Testing	vs.	Result-Driven, Experiential Learning

Millennial Challenges & Solutions

Millennials are smart, passionate, tech savvy, and globally conscious. They're also the first generation since World War II on pace to do worse than their parents in many ways. Rising tuition fees and prerequisite courses can be a major barrier for students hoping to attend the best schools. Wages are too low, technology has replaced jobs, and young professionals are riddled with debt. As Millennials hop from job to job, they sometimes fall into dysfunctional workplaces with "less than professional" peers and employers. In an era with so much opportunity and free information, there's a sense of infinite possibility, but a lack of clear direction. As jobs get more competitive, talent and a degree simply aren't guaranteed calling cards anymore — meaningful results, ethics, happiness, and making a difference matter more than ever.

On my journey, I discovered 4 Essentials that make success not only easier, but far more rewarding. You simply need to connect a few dots. The result will be a real-world MBA — your Master's in Basic Abilities.

The 4 Essentials

1) **Mindset** is the Essential catalyst to any idea, talent, or ability, and a critical bridge to creativity, wealth, and happiness.

2) **Strategies** like focus, leadership, and emotional intelligence are Essential to result-driven people, teams, and companies.

3) **Values** like integrity, humility, and gratitude are Essential to thriving careers, communities, and relationships.

4) **Purpose** principles like passion, friends, health, and making a difference are Essential to your mission and vision (why you do it).

Together, **The 4 Essentials** are not only a game changer in global education, they're a dynamic system for life and business success.

Chapter 1
A Misfit's Journey Begins

> *"Vision is a path to success.*
> *Integrity is the car you drive in.*
> *Beware of forks in the road."*
>
> CLIFF

OSCAR WILDE SAID, "BE yourself, everyone else is taken." To that end, I'll be as candid as possible about my trials and triumphs. I hope this journey inspires you, makes you laugh, helps you think, and even rocks the boat a little. After all, misfits don't always ask permission — sometimes we ask forgiveness.

Personal Disclaimers ...

- I'm semi-dyslexic and a part-time insomniac.
- Love and laughter mean more to me than money.
- I hear better when I listen well. I'm still working on it.
- I learn a lot from mistakes. I plan on making a few more.
- I occasionally make up words. Most stuff is figure-outable.
- I let perfect ruin good sometimes. I don't recommend that.
- I don't think we need a reason to help people — we just should.

Somehow, with all my quirks, I found success and happiness, never regretting failures along the way. Quite often, I was too naïve to know what I couldn't do, so I just did it. That said, if 40-something Cliff could chat with 20-something Cliff, ohhh, the conversations we'd have ...

Childhood Kicks & Chaos

I was born in New York, 1967, the baby brother of two sisters (Gigi and Eve). I was a short, scrawny kid with a gift for gab. That means I was occasionally witty and hard to shut up. My family is Jewish and both parents are from Brooklyn. They divorced as early as I can remember and never spoke again.

My mom was a nurse and dad was a psychiatrist. My father and I shared a common bond of books, sports, and humor, but I only saw him sporadically. Our family moved to Tenafly, New Jersey when I was a baby, and ten more times throughout Los Angeles before I was twelve. As a result, I attended nine schools before I was sixteen.

My sisters and I lived with mom and our childhood was dysfunctional on many levels. Both parents struggled with alcohol, purpose, and emotional discipline. Plenty of kids had a harder life, so my story isn't a tale of tragedy — it's one of chaos, dreams, and growth.

As the youngest, I was oblivious to family squabbles and did my best to tune out the noise. With no family structure from parents, my sisters and I were left to our own devices. Occasionally, I ran away from home for a few days. Gigi and Eve were far more rebellious and left for good in their mid-teens, but they always checked in on me, and for that I'm eternally grateful.

Mostly, I was a home-alone kid, starved for attention. In spite of reading and writing challenges (undiagnosed dyslexia), I was a good student with plenty of time on my hands. Socially awkward, I played a lot of hooky at the beach, local arcade, or bowling ally. No one bothered to ask why I wasn't in school every day, but things were different in the '80s. If necessary, I forged my mom's signature to explain my absence from school, but that was the extent of my shenanigans. Punishment was usually library time and that was fine with me.

It's amazing I didn't get into more trouble, but I was fortunate to be a bookworm (a gift from both parents). I often escaped to my favorite novelists such as Twain, Dickens, Tolkien, and Salinger. Those mentors taught me about humor versus hope, good versus evil, and the inequities of life. They also inspired me to write. Although I'm a slow typist and it took me a decade to write this book, *The 4 Essentials* are my favorite *Cliff Notes*.

I'm also a fan of movies, music, and comedians. My earliest influences were innovators such as Steven Spielberg, Michael Jackson, and Robin Williams. Today, I identify with misfits like Harry Potter, thanks to the genius of author J.K. Rowling. If you're too cool for misfits, stop reading now — there are plenty of books for muggles.

Love & Legacy of The Great Pelé

Growing up, I played a little tennis and baseball, but I dreamed of a professional soccer career from the very first day I laced up my boots. At age 9, I was selected to play for the Los Angeles Junior Aztecs, sponsored by the professional Aztecs of the former North American Soccer League. We even played a few games at Rose Bowl Stadium and trained with international legends such as Johan Cruyff and George Best.

At the time, Brazilian soccer star, Pelé, came out of retirement to play for our cross-country rival, the New York Cosmos. For those who don't know his back-story, Pelé was so poor, his childhood team was known as The Shoeless Ones. As a small boy, he often practiced with grapefruits, but his father (a former soccer professional) taught his son very disciplined practice and team strategies.

In storybook fashion, Pelé was selected to play for Brazil's national team at age 16, and scored six goals in the World Cup. He would ultimately lead Brazil to three World Cup Championships (1958, 1962, 1970). He also led the Cosmos to a championship in 1977. By the end of his career that year, Pelé was the king of soccer with a mind-boggling 1,281 goals.

In his farewell game at Giants Stadium, New York, Pelé suited up one half for the Cosmos and the other for Santos (his native club from Brazil). Before the game, in front of 75,000 screaming fans and a global TV audience, Pelé delivered a short speech about love and kids I would never forget.

"I want to take this opportunity to ask you, in this moment when the world looks to me, to pay more attention to kids all over the world. Love is more important than anything we take from life. Since everything else passes, say with me three times ... LOVE!" ~ PELÉ

An inspired crowd chanted "LOVE!" After the game, world boxing champ Muhammad Ali embraced Pelé and said, "There are now two of The Greatest." I was too young to appreciate the magic in that moment, but Ali and Pelé became two of my greatest mentors. They did more goodwill with messages of love than most world leaders. Deservedly, *TIME Magazine* included both men on their list of "100 Most Important People of the 20th Century."

Months after his farewell game, Pelé appeared at a soccer clinic that I attended with hundreds of youth players. Hoping for an autograph, I shouted out, "What does it take to be a champion?" Pelé flashed his famous smile and shared three magical words, "Practice, teamwork, and love."

Championships & Challenges

By the time I was 11, our Junior Aztecs had won league titles and played goodwill games from England to Israel. As a speedy striker, I had a knack for scoring goals and was asked to play for a club in Liverpool in 1978. It was a rare opportunity for an American youth player, but financially impossible for my family, so the idea was short-lived.

At age 12, I transferred from the Aztecs to our cross town rival, West Valley United. In 1981, we were the first American team to win the largest youth tournament in the world (The Robbie, played annually in Canada). We were heavy underdogs but a scrappy bunch. After defeating a pair of Scottish teams in the quarter and semi-finals, we shocked a heavily favored Canadian club in the finals (4-2). I scored two goals (the tie breaker on a breakaway and game-winner on a diving header). I was 14 that summer and my confidence couldn't be higher.

At 15, injuries began taking their toll. By the time high school rolled around, so did my ankles! By 17, I had torn ligaments and suffered from concussions. Although college scouts showed interest, scholarships went down the drain. In my senior year, physical therapy became routine and new injuries replaced old ones. As an athlete, you know when you've lost your edge.

When high school ended, any hopes of a soccer career were crushed. I spent half my senior year hobbling on crutches, and the other half wondering what I would do with the rest of my life. Emotionally I was lost, but in the corner of my mind, Pelé's wisdom never escaped my soul ...

"Practice, teamwork, and love ..."

9-Year-Old Cliff

Chapter 2
Life 101 & Street Smarts

"Wisdom is not a product of schooling,
but the lifelong attempt to acquire it."
ALBERT EINSTEIN
Theoretical Physicist

A Misfit & His Mentors

I graduated high school a double threat — clueless and penniless. I left home six months before graduation and didn't know where to go. I couldn't afford my own place so I crashed on the couch of whatever friend would have me. The importance of college weighed heavy on my mind. If I decided to go the university route, my father agreed to cover tuition for a year, but I still had to pay for life expenses like car, food, and rent.

I immersed in positive-thinking books but survival strategies were fuzzy at best. Business books provided a few money-making ideas, but I needed real-world experience. I washed cars and painted houses for a little cash, but after reading entrepreneur magazines, real estate intrigued me the most.

With my pockets full of nothing but ambition, I walked into open houses and asked realtors how to buy and sell homes. Most of them laughed at my ripped jeans, but a few investors let me tag along. I drove them crazy with a million questions, so they gave me a full-time job as a gopher. Whatever they needed from copies to coffee, I hustled and learned. The gig only paid $100 dollars per week, but it was the street-smart experience I needed.

My real estate mentors bought and sold properties that usually needed some rehab. I was up at 7:00 a.m. each day to search newspapers for bargains. By 9:00 a.m., I started making calls to owners, agents, and banks. By noon, I would wolf down a brown-bag lunch and go door-knocking to analyze homes. It was a great way to learn about cash-flow, property values, and remodeling costs. With each deal, I picked up keys to negotiation such as a seller's motivation, terms, and conditions. My mentors also taught me the difference between chasing good deals and avoiding bad ones. In return for their wisdom, they expected me to be well-organized on each property (lot size, square footage, comparable sales, and the homeowner's story). I soon realized that the big dogs needed little hounds like me to sniff out the best deals.

I wanted to keep working full-time, but that would be a challenge if I left for college, so my mentors offered a more flexible weekend job with an extra kicker. If I could find a deal 25% below market, they agreed to help me buy my own property. In the interim, I'd still get paid to hunt deals that met their criteria (15% below market). I accepted the challenge, knowing I might hear "No" a hundred times before "Yes." Sure enough, there were a ton of rejections, but I also cultivated a network of seasoned realtors and bankers who sent daily deals for my mentors to consider. It was a rapid-fire, real-world education and I was incredibly grateful that so many strangers were willing to teach the ropes to a wet-behind-the-ears teenager.

The Core Essentials

1) Say "Thank You" ... a lot!
2) Time is our most valuable asset
3) The future depends on today's focus
4) Care the most to create win-win scenarios

Those early lessons were priceless, but of all the habits I learned that summer, handwritten thank-you notes were the number one secret to building relationships. My mentors never went home before sending letters to clients and prospects (no e-mails back then). My personal touch was to leave a business card, chocolate kiss, and thank-you note on each broker's desk (and every homeowner's door step). Before long, they called me the Hershey-Kisses Kid.

As the fall semester approached, I asked my dad if he'd still pay for a year of college. He agreed, as long as I covered my other expenses. I figured if money as a house painter and gopher lasted long enough, I'd find that elusive bargain property, make a bundle of cash, and all would be well in my world.

Okay college ... here I come!

Chapter 3
A Unique College Experience

> *"I never let my schooling*
> *interfere with my education."*
> MARK TWAIN
> Humorist, Novelist

In Search of Education & Entrepreneurship

IN THE FALL OF 1985, I enrolled at the University of Southern California (USC). I was the freshman nerd with a *Wall Street Journal* under one arm and a business book under the other. I wanted to look like I belonged in this strange new world, but for all intents and purposes, I was still a misfit. I never joined a campus club because my anxiety about money left me with just enough sanity to work and study. Although I was learning life lessons on the street, I was missing all the fun of a college experience.

I initially loved the idea of going to USC, but it wasn't long before reality set in. After classes each day, I painted houses, but that barely covered the bills. I soon became an insomniac, wondering how I would ever balance work, school, a social life, and a checkbook. The lack of sleep also made it difficult to pay attention in class, so when I asked professors for flexible schedules, they looked at me with utter disdain. By the end of my freshman year, I was at a financial and emotional crossroads. My lease was up, my spirit was down, and I had paint on half my clothes. If I didn't find a way to make more money or cut expenses, it was time to quit college.

And then I got the call ...

7

Persistence Pays Off

A month before my sophomore year at USC, I received a call from a homeowner named Kate who I met the previous year when I started hunting bargain properties. Kate was selling a 2-bedroom Hollywood Hills condo and promised to stay in touch if she ever dropped her price.

I followed up each month with a friendly note and chocolate kiss. When she finally reached out, Kate was six months behind mortgage payments and her bank was ready to foreclose. The condo was a rental property that she and her brother inherited, but they hated being landlords. When it was time to sell, the first person she and her brother called was the kid who left all those letters and kisses at the front door!

"Cliff, we've neglected the condo for years, but if you and your investor can purchase by the end of the month, you'd be doing us a huge favor. If the deal goes through, you'll save our credit, and I think you'll make money in the long run. The condo just needs some love!" said Kate. That was an "aha" moment for me because it proved that a deal could be a win-win for both parties.

I knew it wouldn't be an overnight success and the condo needed major fixes, but I pitched it to my favorite mentor Bill and he liked the deal enough to jump right in. The original asking price was $120,000 dollars, but we negotiated a final price of $90,000 (25% below market). The deal required a down payment of $4,500 dollars (which I thought was a lot of money), but Bill just smiled and said, "Piece of cake."

The result was a victory for Kate because the bank promised to clean up her credit if the deal closed within a month (which it did). It was a win for Bill because I agreed to live in the property, make repairs, and give Bill 25% of future profits. It was a win for me because I was just 19 and bought my first home. Even if the property didn't increase in value, it would be a potential nest egg when college was over.

In less than thirty days, I moved in, painted the condo, rented the extra bedroom to classmates, and that's how I solved my biggest cash-flow problem. Back on campus, friends wanted to know how I pulled off a real estate deal on a student budget. Most of us were scrambling for lunch money, so when word got out about my bachelor pad, I was labeled, "The Lucky Landlord!"

Sure, there was some luck, but if my mentors didn't encourage me to follow routines, and write thank-you notes each day, I doubt I'd be telling this story ...

My "Lucky" Routine

- Planning & persistence
- Dozens of calls per day
- Face-to-face networking
- Learning & creative thinking
- Daily thank-you notes & kisses

As I explained my daily routine to friends, it was apparent that street-smart routines were as valuable as any high school or college course we had taken. Everyone needed to master *Essential* skills like budgets, networking, project planning, and the subtle art of thank-you notes. "Get me the university President!" I shouted. "I'm blowing this story wide open!"

But I digress. I was 19, full of passion and conspiracy theories.
Maybe my little condo was dumb luck and I still had a lot to learn.

The Boat Rockers

My bigger goal was to attend USC's entrepreneur program. It was ahead of its time in the '80s and still ranks as one of the top schools in America today. There were a few leadership courses in the undergraduate program, but the business school had more tedious prerequisites like statistics and economics. How can I say this nicely — just shoot me now! As a dyslexic kid, math was torture. It was like telling a violinist he had to take prerequisite hockey. If mastery of spreadsheets was the measure of my talent, my days at USC were numbered.

A few friends were blessed with wealthy families or scholarships that made schools like USC affordable, but most students I knew didn't have the grades or money to attend elite universities. With my college days on the brink due to financial strains, I started asking everyone how important they felt it was to get a degree. There were four answers: 1) College is about the experience, not the degree; 2) A degree is essential to certain professions and a well-rounded education; 3) A degree shows your ability to go the distance; 4) A degree won't matter at all to some careers.

My head was now spinning, insomnia got worse, and grades were suffering. One afternoon, I was eating lunch on the campus lawn, listening to students and professors argue about prerequisite courses and skyrocketing tuition fees. The friendly dialogue reached a fever pitch around one critical question ...

9

> Do high schools, colleges, and career-training programs
> offer enough essentials for real-world success?

To properly address the issue, we created a weekly coffee chat. A group of us discussed everything from "progressive curriculums" to the wildest idea of "no tuition for non-essential courses." From freshman to seniors, we saw ourselves as boat rockers who might even start a campus revolution. A few of the open-minded professors were genuinely interested in our views, but we were never sure if they were with us, or just indulging us. By the middle of my sophomore year, those talks got a bit confrontational, even though everyone agreed about gaps in the education system.

Business majors and creative artists felt undergraduate programs placed too much emphasis on courses like calculus and accounting. STEM majors (science, tech, engineering, math) didn't want arts and language classes taking up critical-thinking time. Long semesters didn't favor attention-deficit kids, and if tuition fees weren't enough, each school charged hundreds of dollars for text books. The biggest epiphany was that a college experience (like high school) was only as good as the teacher you were lucky enough to get. For example, a teacher once asked me if we were on the same page and I said, "I'm not even sure we're reading the same book!"

I was fortunate to have one professor who provided the inspiration to my underground college thesis (*Essentials Critical to Life & Career Success*). He was failing me for missing too many classes, but allowed me to conduct an extra-credit survey to improve my grade. I ended up polling over 300 people from all walks of life (artists, athletes, scientists, parents, teachers, business leaders, high school students, college graduates). I asked everyone to rank *Essentials* they would use to hire employees or identify promising entrepreneurs.

Nearly every respondent said grades and degrees were indicators of hard work, but those factors rated no higher than talent, passion, mindset, and experience. Among the highest-rated assets were focus, teamwork, leadership, problem solving, creative-thinking, communication, and people skills. Values such as integrity, humility, and gratitude were critical to employers. In short, the top students, professors, CEOs, and entrepreneurs confirmed that dozens of *Essentials* were absent from high school, college, and corporate training, especially when students are most vulnerable. The results begged a serious question:

> If success is determined in large part by real-world Essentials,
> doesn't logic dictate we teach them at the earliest possible age?

Final Grade on My Education Theory

In the winter of 1986, I shared the survey results with my professor. He agreed not to fail me (which was nice), but disagreed with my theory. He said, "Students could only learn so much in a classroom and that most *Essentials* had to be experienced in the real world." I agreed in part, but I also made the case that his premise was flawed. How do we explain intelligent people who repeat the same mistakes even with years of experience? Many professionals are heavily influenced by dysfunctional peers, teachers, and employers. We can't learn from failure if we're not even sure how to identify problems. Individuals and teams need the right environments to exploit their talents. In short, my radical theory back in the '80s is just as relevant today.

> "Experience doesn't always teach success principles. It may only teach what not to do. The 4 Essentials (mindset, strategies, values, purpose) should therefore be part of every education and career-training program."

I asked my professor if he would discuss the survey results with university leaders. He just smiled and pointed to the chalkboard where a business lesson was scribed in big letters: **Opportunity Cost = The value of one experience at the expense of another**. In that moment, I was just a 19-year-old troublemaker getting smacked down for speaking up. I then calculated the cost of staying in college (the only math I knew), and that was my last day at USC.

Years later, I regretted leaving because I could have learned so much more and networked with amazing people. I always say that anyone with the means or motive to enjoy college should do it, but for those who can't, your future is not solely determined by a degree. There's abundant opportunity for anyone to fulfill their passion and purpose.

In my case, a lack of money and bag of personal issues sent me packing. Nonetheless, I cherished my time at USC and was proud of the debate between us misfits and the establishment. We rocked the boat a little and I've always thought that was a good thing. As I walked off campus, I was intimidated by what I bargained for, but hopeful that my unique experience would provide a real-world MBA (**M**aster's in **B**asic **A**bilities).

Fight on Trojans! Hello crazy world ...

11

Chapter 4
Welcome to The Real World

> *"We learn by example and by direct experience because there are real limits to the adequacy of verbal instruction."*
> MALCOLM GLADWELL
> Bestselling Author

My Leap Without a Parachute

I WAS JUST 19 and had no college degree or safety net if things didn't work out, but I arrived just in time for the real-estate boom of the late '80s. Then in 1988 (age 21), I sold my Hollywood Hills condo at the height of the market, paid off Bill, and used my share of profits to buy two more properties. With ideas from architecture magazines, I learned to fix up homes. The first one went off without a hitch. On the second one, I discovered all the little things that could go wrong — like earthquakes, plumbing headaches, and contractor surprises that would cost twice as much time and money than expected.

In spite of those hard knocks, I finally had enough cash for dating and a new car. I studied at night to get my real estate broker's license and went to work for a prominent company in Sherman Oaks, California. For a few years, I helped dozens of friends and clients buy, sell, and finance homes. I was one of the firm's top producers and life as a college dropout couldn't be better. By 1990 however, the real estate market crashed and I was in over my head with too many homes and headaches. Years of blood, sweat, and tears went down the drain in just a few months.

Welcome to the real world, big shot!

Rookie Lessons Learned

The '89-'90 real estate crash taught me a ton of lessons. I tried to be too many things to all people, including myself. Investor. Landlord. Realtor. Mortgage broker. Remodeling junkie! Like many people in the '80s, I bit off more than I could chew, and failed miserably at the one rule every mentor taught me — FOCUS!

Although I had lost everything, I was eager to start my own real estate company. Friends thought I was nuts to even think of it in a bad market, but mentors always told me, "In good times or bad, people need help." That was especially true when it came to buying, selling, and financing homes. Sure enough, my phone kept ringing and deals were coming my way. Sending thank-you notes never stopped paying off. Was I ready to start my own company? Probably not, but misfits usually trust their gut.

So in 1991, age 24, I took another crazy leap ...!

Think Big or Die Hard

If buying my first condo in college was a stroke of luck, negotiating my first office was a bowl of Lucky Charms. I had very little cash after the market tumbled, but in hopes of gaining a competitive edge, I chose an office location at The Fox Plaza on Avenue of the Stars, one of the most luxurious skyscrapers in Century City, Los Angeles. Movie fans may recall this tower from the 1988 Bruce Willis film, *Die Hard* (Nakatomi Plaza). The intriguing part of this story is how we got rent-free office space in that building!

The person who taught me creative negotiation tactics was a lawyer named Kim. I helped her find a new home and ended up buying her lunch each week to pick her brain about lease and purchase contracts. I told Kim I wanted an office, but had a tight budget. She suggested I make an offer to sublease space in the nicest building, then trade my services for free rent. I thought the idea was farfetched but I gave it a shot. I called every leasing agent in town, until an attorney named Dave heard my proposal. A mutual acquaintance told him I was a hard-working young broker trying to catch a break.

Dave told me he had just signed a lease for 10,000 square feet in the Fox Plaza. Unfortunately, the merger of his small firm to a bigger company fell apart, and he was stuck with all that empty space! Dave said, "Cliff, my partners and I buy a lot of real estate. If you agree not to charge full commissions and do the first few deals free, you can be our broker. I'll give you 1000 square feet of free space and will only charge you $400 for parking." Before saying yes, I asked if we could use some of the phones, copy machines, leather chairs, and mahogany desks that were just collecting dust in the office. Dave winked and said, "You've got guts kid — it's a deal!" I could barely sleep that night. Getting a furnished office in the most famous building in town was a jackpot for any startup.

With all those expenses saved, I hired a transaction coordinator and began working around the clock. The occasional pro bono work for Dave and his partners was no big deal. I was getting plenty of referrals by networking in the building. Everyone from bankers and wealth managers to famous entertainers had an office in our building. Naturally, they all got a bag of chocolate kisses at their front desk, courtesy of Cliff Michaels & Associates. It was the best two dollars I spent each day. My team and I also helped Dave rent out the rest of his empty space, so he stopped charging us for parking. Voilà! That's how I launched "rent free" in the famous Fox Plaza.

In Vegas they say, "Go Big or Go Home."
Dave was fond of saying, "Think Big or Die Hard."
I never forgot that lesson.

Do You Know The Muffin Man?

After opening my real estate and mortgage firm in 1992, I focused on the high-profile demographic that was prevalent on Avenue of the Stars. Answering calls morning to midnight, I gained a reputation as a conscientious broker. At the opening of each deal, I scheduled lunch with a client and their brain trust (agents, spouses, attorneys, accountants, financial planners, business managers, insurance brokers). In most cases, a client's financial entourage had rarely met in person as a group, so they appreciated the work luncheons I arranged. The camaraderie also generated a ton of business for everyone.

Thriving in competitive waters wasn't as complicated as business schools made it sound. My team and I simply focused on clients, not the competition. We treated people like family. My most cost-effective marketing strategy was sending a muffin or wine basket to each buyer, seller, or agent at the start *and* end of each deal. I learned early in the game that people were friendlier with muffins or a bottle of wine on their desk.

On one occasion, I dropped off a muffin basket and a dozen pizzas to a competitive banker's staff who helped one of my clients close a deal while I was out of town. He appreciated the gesture so much that he asked me to train his sales team. I soon conducted workshops that included sales training, networking, negotiations, and time management. My banking and real estate pals didn't learn these *Essentials* in school either, but once they mastered gift baskets and

15

thank-you notes, their sales went through the roof! Suddenly, my nickname went from the Hershey-Kisses Kid to The Muffin Man!

By 29, business was solid. For the most part, I was a happy camper. However, serious bouts with insomnia returned for the first time since college. I was suffering from burnout and probably in denial about how unbalanced my life really was. It wasn't just a matter of all-work-and-no-play. I *craved* a more creative outlet and meaningful purpose. So I asked a few colleagues to cover for me, and decided on a long-overdue sabbatical.

Where's The Reset Button?

By the mid-nineties, my real estate team and I shifted gears and worked from home. Who needs an office when you've got e-mail and computers? I hated tech but everyone encouraged me to get on board the digital train. I wasn't ready for the dot-com world so I spent most of my vacation time on a golf course, tennis court, or yoga mat. Between fairways, backhands, and warrior poses, I asked friends about the meaning of life. They told me to read the Dalai Lama's *Art of Happiness,* and it helped me find the reset button, but I was still crawling the entrepreneurial walls of my mind.

So much for meditation.
After six months off, I needed a fresh focus.
The Internet was a popular new toy. Maybe that was worth exploring ...?

21-Year-Old Cliff

A Brave, New World

Chapter 5
Diary of a Dot-com

> *"Twenty years from now you will be more disappointed*
> *by the things you didn't do than the ones you did.*
> *So throw off the bowlines. Sail away from safe harbor.*
> *Catch the trade winds in your sails. Explore, Dream. Discover."*
> MARK TWAIN

Young Entrepreneurs

AT A CROSSROADS WITH many business ideas in my late twenties, I joined the Young Entrepreneurs' Organization (YEO, known today as EO). EO is still the world's premier network for young business owners, providing peer-to-peer learning through chapter events, private forums, and global leadership conferences. The organization had less than 1,000 members when I joined, but by 2016 EO had over 12,000 members with 120 chapters in over 50 countries.

I sat on the YEO Los Angeles Board from 1996 to 2004. As chapter President, I helped chair international events and launched our first student mentor programs at local high schools and universities. I also chaired our first L.A. philanthropic events for kids at risk and physically-challenged youth.

In those early days, I was incredibly humbled by fellow members who had innovative companies around the world. I was just a real estate guy in Los Angeles, searching for new ways to balance life, and maybe rock the boat with a big idea. I had no sooner attended a YEO Global Learning Conference, when my peers challenged me to think big. "You're a passionate guy, Cliff!" they said. "Why not jump on the Internet and launch one of those pioneering dot-com companies?"

That sounded simple enough ...

Hatching a Big Idea (summer, 1996)

In 2001, I wrote a book titled *Diary of a Dot-com*. It chronicled the roller-coaster ride of a pioneering Internet startup that I co-founded in the late '90s. I never published the original story for a host of reasons. You'll get the gist after reading this Cliff-Note edition, written ten years after the fact.

I always wanted to do something for global education with *The 4 Essentials*. The Internet seemed like a perfect venue, so in the summer of '96 I launched a website called Knowledge Café. At the time, Amazon.com was starting out as the Earth's Biggest Book Store. I thought I'd carve out a niche for myself by selling career and entrepreneur programs based on my live workshops. I was so naïve about those early Internet days that I e-mailed Amazon's founder Jeff Bezos to ask if he was looking for a partner. He never wrote back, but I went forward with Knowledge Café and it became a fun, online community for entrepreneurs. My sister Gigi and her husband Craig Honick helped me design my first website. They were building e-commerce platforms in the mid '90s before most people had an e-mail address. Just as I was ramping up Knowledge Café, I got a late-night call from Craig that piqued my interest.

CRAIG: "Cliff, I have a game-changing idea for an Internet company."

CLIFF: "Game-changing? Please share!"

CRAIG: "I'm building a website for a lawyer who wants to know if web developers have a method to register "first use" of their ideas, such as music, videos, or artwork. There will soon be millions of websites and a billion people sharing digital content online so he's identified a unique, global problem."

CLIFF: "That's a lot of files. Where are you going with this?"

CRAIG: "If you had a screenplay, invention, or important legal record, and wanted irrefutable time-sealed evidence of what you created, how would you prove it?"

CLIFF: "I suppose I would get a notary, copyright, patent, or trademark."

CRAIG: "Right, but even notarized documents and computer files can be altered after they're created, so the chain of evidence inherently lacks trust."

CLIFF: "So what's the big idea?"

CRAIG: "Imagine an Internet registry that could timestamp and authenticate the world's files the moment they're created. Think of it as a digital online notary."

CLIFF: "Interesting. How do we build such a thing?"

CRAIG: "I'm not sure, but imagine the possibilities if we could."

At the time, Craig was a college professor teaching economics at Cal State Northridge. At UCLA, he was also working on his Ph.D. in organizational change, so he understood why his digital-notary idea was on a collision course with the Internet boom. In 1996, there were less than 250 million personal computers, but projected growth told a different story. By the year 2000, there were 738 million Internet users (three billion users by 2016). As actor Justin Timberlake said in the movie *The Social Network* (portraying Facebook Co-Founder Sean Parker), "This is a once-in-a-lifetime-holy-shit idea!"

Excited about the opportunity, I sold Knowledge Café and began brainstorming with Craig. We started looking at revenue models based on what we thought our target customer might pay for a digital notary (such as a monthly subscription for unlimited files, or maybe a dollar for individual files). If you consider all the e-mails, websites, digital records, online transactions, and intellectual property bouncing around, it's easy to see why Craig's idea was a game-changer.

As a first layer of time-sealed ownership proof, a digital notary would be far less expensive than a $10 notary, $20 copyright, or the thousands of dollars traditionally paid for patents or trademarks. Best of all, clients could instantly notarize unlimited files, in any language, from anywhere in the world. Any way we sliced it, this wasn't just a million-dollar idea — it was a billion-dollar beast!

Like many dot-com virgins, neither Craig nor I had run a technology company. We were inspired however by famous tech tandems like Gates and Allen (Microsoft) or Jobs and Wozniak (Apple), and the latest Internet giants like Google, Pay Pal, and GoDaddy. Maybe we were on to the next big thing?

After our initial brainstorm, Craig and I mapped out a monthly strategy. If we ever actually launched the idea, my job would be to raise capital and lead a sales team. Craig's job would be to build the website and find a secure time stamp method. We weren't sure how the start-up money would magically appear, but everyone seemed to be raising capital for ground-breaking technology. Why not us?

The Company Solution

We called the company First Use for its dual meaning: 1) your ability to prove when you first created a file, and 2) First Use is a legal term for proving claims to intellectual property. At FirstUse.com, we built the world's first online registry with software applications that featured a digital notary.

How A Digital Notary Works

Microsoft Word File

New
Open ...
Save

Digital Notary with FirstUse.com
Verify Files with FirstUse.com

Page Setup...
Print Preview
Print...

Let's say you wanted to create a logo, screenplay, software code, or legal document in your favorite software program. Our website enabled you to have us notarize any size or type of file (text, audio, video, photo). The same way a human fingerprint is unique to a person, our service could generate a digital fingerprint of a file, enabling users to send that fingerprint over the Internet, have it time-stamped by FirstUse.com, and stored with a user's account information. A digital fingerprint is also known as a one-way hash code and looks like this: **ABCDF_165a373rp754tfz007gk54fdgdd.**

First Use • Digital Notary Certificate

File Name: Screenplay Draft, Version 21
Registrant: John Doe • File #: 6547564723
Address: 123 Dream Street, Los Angeles, California, 90049
File's Digital Fingerprint: ABCDF_165a373rp754tfz007gk54fdgdd
Registered Date & Time: 12/31/99, 11:59:30 p.m. GMT

The Legal Power of Math

The world is made up of many laws and languages, but math is the only universal standard that can resolve disputes with scientific certainty. Simply stated, our niche was a digital-notary signature based on math! Our service wasn't a substitute for legal registration like copyrights, trademarks, or patents, but something far more valuable — a tamper-proof, time-sealed audit trail of what you created, when you created it, and that files were never altered after the fact.

Pre-Launch Planning (spring, 1997 - spring 1998)

To attract venture capital, we started with homework on cyber law and our target market. Our first visit was to my attorney Jay Patel, who looked at us as if we had discovered plutonium. "This is a big idea guys. If you can do what you think you can, raise capital fast!" said Jay. Every lawyer we spoke to shared Jay's enthusiasm.

By early 1998, we had written a great business plan and Craig designed a beta website to show investors, but we still needed software coders to build a digital-notary. Fortunately, my tech pal Tony East knew exactly what we had in mind and the brainpower to make it happen (Tony is one of those math wizards like Matt Damon's character in the movie *Good Will Hunting*). The good news according to Tony was that it would be relatively easy to build a digital-notary service if we developed a secure time-stamp method. The bad news was that if we could do it, so could someone else, and for months we worried about how it would suck if some monster company beat us to the punch.

They Did? Un-Freaking-Believable! (summer, 1998)

Two years after we originally had the idea, we discovered a patented technology that originated in the early '90s at Bellcore Labs (a spin-off of AT&T). It was run by a firm called Surety Technologies and provided the most cryptographically secure time-stamp in the world — conveniently named DIGITAL NOTARY™!

Surety intended to market their time-stamping solution to big players who owned tons of data, such as banks, governments, and pharmaceutical companies. The upshot was that no one we spoke to had ever heard of Surety. Since our idea for a global registry could make their technology more accessible to consumers and big companies alike, it was clear that we were as much a threat to them as they were a potential partner for us. On one hand, we could be sued if we infringed on their patents. On the other hand, we had nothing to lose if we called, just to see what Surety's reaction might be.

Thankfully, Surety saw us a distribution channel to millions of writers, lawyers, creative artists, and small business owners, so we jumped on a plane to visit their headquarters in New Jersey. They were friendly, but their marketing pitch would have baffled a rocket scientist. As it turned out, their brochure was written by a rocket scientist and that's why it was confusing. After just one meeting, Surety was so impressed with the simplicity of our pitch, they granted us worldwide rights to their Digital Notary™. If successful, we would pay them a small licensing fee. If we failed, it was no skin off anyone's nose.

Raising Venture Capital (autumn, 1998)

The Surety deal saved us a year in development and a fortune in startup costs. We also gained instant credibility with lawyers and tech experts. It was now time to raise venture capital. We needed $300,000 dollars to go to market. Our bigger goal was to raise $5 million dollars, but none of the venture capital firms (VCs) thought we were ready. We didn't have a seasoned management team, nor did we have proof that clients would actually pay. However, after a year of rejections from VCs, there was a ton of media buzz around cyber law, how to manage digital files on the Internet, and disputes over intellectual property like creative designs and software codes. By late 1998, that buzz helped us raise $300,000 dollars in venture capital with angel investors and seasoned entrepreneurs.

Our angels only had one major funding condition which we didn't think much of at the time. They insisted on hiring a CEO who had launched companies for them before (although he had never launched an Internet company). We were so new to the venture capital game that we happily gave up 33% of our company to the investors, including 8% of company stock to our new CEO. We were far more concerned with introducing the world's first Digital Notary™ than who got to wear the CEO hat!

The Launch (October, 1998)

With seed capital in hand, we launched First Use in October of 1998. Things were exciting at first, but software bugs, legal fees, and staffing issues immediately burned capital in ways we never imagined. A bigger issue was that our CEO only showed up a few hours each day while the rest of us were burning the midnight oil. He would soon admit to having trouble at home and no time for his role. Our Board of Directors unanimously voted to terminate his contract just a few months after we launched. It was a costly error, and temporarily pulled the wind from our sails, but we took our medicine and moved on fast.

The most *Essential* lessons from our rocky start were: 1) be sure to hire people who share your values and work ethic; 2) always screen personal and professional references carefully, regardless of who referred them; and 3) set performance benchmarks with timelines and accountability for everyone.

Craig and I took over as Co-CEOs and started chasing more capital. At the time, we were also speaking at Internet conferences and made a strong impression on many industries starved for time-stamping and file-authentication solutions. Concurrently, our sales team was signing strategic alliances with major trade associations in legal, tech, and entertainment. This attracted clients from over 70 countries such as lawyers, scientists, and creative artists. We weren't famous, but a Digital Notary™ Registry was a game changer in a new and crazy Internet world!

Media Buzz (Q1, 1999)

First Use Online Registry
Launches World's First Digital Notary™

Entrepreneur Magazine • Law Technology News •

Los Angeles Times • Business 2.0

Success Magazine • Daily Variety • Forrester Research

Branding Trust (spring, 1999)

Even with a little media buzz, VCs still wanted assurance that our Digital Notary™ would hold up in a real-world dispute, so we fortified our brand with legal and political power. We added a prominent Washington DC lawyer to our team named Andrew Sherman, general counsel for the Young Entrepreneurs' Organization. Andrew was an expert on digital and intellectual property law, and represented major Internet companies like America Online. Andrew also introduced us to Meryl Marshall, Chairwoman for The Academy of Television Arts and Sciences, and a former lawyer who helped us form an alliance with The Academy.

Another influential attorney added to our team was Michael Brown, whose father Ron Brown was Secretary of Commerce during Bill Clinton's Presidency. Michael arranged a White House meeting where Craig and I presented Digital Notary™ to chief technology advisors of President Clinton and Vice President Al Gore. We also met leaders of Congress, the Copyright Office, and the Patent

Office who said that First Use might even be "The Standard for a Digital Notary™," but they also asked an insightful question that caught us by surprise. "Would our services be ready for the Millennium Bug on January 1, 2000?"

Holy crap! We were so caught up in our big idea, we didn't think about a global crisis that was brewing in 1999 — the Y2K problem (aka: the Millennium Bug). As the year came to a dramatic close, panic attacks broke out worldwide. Banks, individuals, and Internet companies feared that computer clocks might not decipher the year 2000 from the year 1900 in the new Millennium.

A Race Against The Clock (Q2-Q4, 1999)

Our first-to-market position as Digital-Notary™ pioneers gave us a leg up on the whole Y2K conversation and potential competitors. That subtle advantage enabled us to raise an additional $3 million dollars from a few more angel investors and a venture capital firm. It came shortly after we fired our CEO in early 1999, and as it turned out, we needed every penny!

As Internet start-ups moved at light speed to be the next big thing, the danger of falling behind was very real. To that end, our new investors asked us to focus more on corporate clients (a target for larger revenue). So we shifted gears from being a simple B2C model (business-to-consumer), and turned most of our attention to the B2B model (business-to-business). It was like driving 100 miles per hour, turning on a dime, and picking up hitch hikers! The risk with such a big move was trying to be all things to all people. It was easy to lose focus and burn capital that way — sure enough, we did. Craig and I even had to stop taking salaries. By late 1999, it was a race against the clock (and our dwindling bank account)!

By early 2000, we were bleeding cash. It was time to raise the $5 million dollars we hoped for at the start. The alternatives were to sell our company, find a partner, or quit. Craig and I fired up the venture-capital road show one more time and pitched everyone who would listen. After many rejections, I got a call from a venture fund at Ernst & Young (EY), a global powerhouse in business consulting who were impressed with First Use. After a month of due diligence, they proposed a $5-million-dollar round of capital.

That same month, we also had an offer from a Silicon Valley VC who wanted to include RSA (a world leader in encryption) as a potential partner. So in the span of thirty days, we went from the brink of no investor prospects to negotiating multiple offers. EY even said our company might be worth $100 million dollars if we hit milestones within a few years. As our lawyers and VCs discussed price and terms for months, I began having panic attacks and slept very little.

Craig and I weren't sure if we'd still own much of the company when all was said and done, but with so many loyal clients and investors relying on us, we didn't want to let anyone down.

Dot-Com or Dot-Bomb? (January-April, 2000)

In early months of the year 2000, there was a funky vibe around Internet startups.

1) Did all those new dot-coms deserve such enormous valuations, even though they had little revenue in a fast-growth world?

2) Were banks and venture capitalists taking on too much risk, handing over multi-million-dollar start-up checks to rookie CEOs?

Tic-Toc-Dramaville ... Craig and I were on pins and needles as negotiations dragged on from New Year's Day to April. After years of blood, sweat, and tears, our team was certain that a deal was just a few days away. Then in the spring of 2000, the dot-com bubble burst, venture capital dried up, and thousands of online companies around the world heard the deafening sound of DOT-BOMB!

We continued to bootstrap all year, doing everything in our power to merge with a partner, get new funding, or sell the company, but the market crash made First Use just another footnote in the history of pioneering Internet companies. No glory. No headlines. Game over.

These days, secure, digital time-stamping is part of many software applications and online platforms. When Craig and I see how far Digital-Notary™ services have come since the late '90s, all we can do is smile and say, "Yep, we started that back in the Wild West West of the Worldwide Web — a dollar short and maybe a decade ahead of our time."

What Worked Best

Passion, purpose, and teamwork were amazing at First Use. Craig and I learned something new each day from people much smarter than us, enabling us to create a solution to a global challenge. That vision enabled us to raise millions of dollars and develop clients in 70 countries. When things went wrong, everyone worked around the clock with a core belief that we could make a difference. Our legacy to the legal and digital world is that we rocked the boat and raised the bar for digital-notary services, even though we failed as a company.

What Didn't Work

We often let perfect ruin good and didn't realize how much time and money could be wasted if things went sideways. We may have gone much further had we focused on small consumers or big corporations, but not both at the same time. If you don't have focus and revenue, you won't have a viable business for long, no matter how much capital you raise. If we could do it over, we would have engaged more experienced partners and start-up investors, but hindsight is always 20/20.

A Path to Greater Purpose

There's no doubt First Use made me a stronger entrepreneur, but my biggest lesson was more about self awareness. When we launched, I loved the idea of solving a global challenge. Within months however, I knew I wasn't doing something I loved. I missed helping clients on a personal level. I was a misfit who had lost his way.

Then, in the spring of 2000 as the market crashed, our family suffered an even greater loss. My 16-year-old niece Jenny was killed in a car accident. She was an honor student, dancer, and beautiful soul who always made me laugh. The silver lining came in a few words she wrote in a poem titled *LIFE*. The first eight words are all you need to know: **"Stop. Take a breath. Set aside your life."**

Later that year, I took time off to reflect on things that mattered most (health, friends, and family). In years to follow, I devoted more time to my greatest passions, like mentoring students and coaching entrepreneurs. Something felt really good about helping those who were eager to make their mark on the world. By 2007, I had written over 100 essays on my favorite mentors, past and present. Before I knew it, I had dozens of stories and systems for life and business that fit into *4 Essential* categories: *Mindset, Strategies, Values, Purpose*. That same year, I gave away all my worldly possessions and took a sabbatical to South East Asia. Inspired by Jenny, friends, and clients, I outlined this book on a white-sand beach with a mission to inspire, give back, and raise the bar for global education.

In 2012, I was humbled to see *The 4 Essentials* launch #1 on Amazon and #3 on the New York Times Bestseller List (originally titled: *The 4 Essentials of Entrepreneurial Thinking*). A few months later, I was invited to share my story and *The 4 Essentials* at USC's top entrepreneur class. It was a surreal moment for a kid like me who dropped out of college two decades earlier. Extra thanks go to USC Professors Dave Belasco, Patrick Henry, and Dave Logan for letting me know misfits can always come home. I guess my professor back in the '80s was right all along — some things we only learn through experience.

My Journey Continues

In 2013, I was planning a book tour, but suffered a series of sports injuries that put my plans on hold (back, knee, shoulder). It all stemmed from scoliosis (a curved spine), so I guess my body is a misfit too!

In 2014, I was limping by a pet rescue center near my house, and spotted a puppy who was struggling to walk. The shelter told me this scrawny beagle-mix had a virus, and only a 5% chance of survival. I named her Lucy and took her home. With good food, daily walks, and tons of love, we were both healed within a year. You might say we rescued each other. The doctors called her The Miracle Mutt, but I call her Lucy The Warrior Pup!

In late 2016, I released the 2nd Edition of *The 4 Essentials* and designed a series of e-learning programs to compliment lessons in this book. I also facilitate forums and live retreats for students, professionals, and entrepreneurs worldwide, so please let me know if I can help your team, school, or company. You can learn more at CliffMichaels.com.

With gratitude,
Namaste and seize the day!

Cliff & Lucy

Your Essential Journey Begins

In the following chapters, we'll have fun with misfits and mentors who teach us what successful people didn't learn in school. The 4 Essentials will also help you graduate life with a real-world MBA — your **Master's** in **Basic Abilities**!

Essential 1 · **Mindset**

*"Every great wizard in history started out as a student.
If they can do it, why not us?"*

DANIEL RADCLIFFE (HARRY POTTER)
Actor (Misfit Wizard)

Align Your Essentials

WHETHER YOU'RE AN ARTIST, athlete, scientist, or CEO, *Essential 1 (Mindset)* should always be aligned with *Essential 2 (Strategies), Essential 3 (Values)*, and *Essential 4 (Purpose)*. Although I firmly believe in positive thinking, my challenge to you is to go beyond self-help mantras. When you connect a specific mindset to proven success systems, you'll drive much greater results in your life, career, and business.

Master These 5 Mindsets

Mindset 1) Define Success & Happiness
Mindset 2) Unleash Your Entrepreneurial Soul
Mindset 3) Cultivate Creative Thinking
Mindset 4) Build a Result-Driven Practice
Mindset 5) Show Grit & Never Quit

Mindset 1
Define Success & Happiness

> *"Success is liking yourself,*
> *liking what you do, and liking how you do it."*
> MAYA ANGELOU
> Poet, Historian, Activist

How Would You Describe The Good Life?

- Love & Laughter
- Friends & Family
- A Rewarding Career
- Fame & Financial Freedom
- A Healthy Mind, Body & Soul
- Making a Difference in the World

There's a famous parable about how we define success and happiness. It's been written by poets in many languages with themes that range from a pirate's tale to a Buddhist myth. The most modern version is titled *The Good Life* (2009), originally known as *The Mexican Fisherman* (1996), both written by Dr. Mark Albion, a former professor at Harvard Business School. When I told Mark I was writing *The 4 Essentials*, he graciously endorsed my version of the famous fisherman's tale. The story is a great way to start people on their journey by posing a simple question, "How would you describe The Good Life?"

If you're not sure, ask Harvard Joe and the Fisherman ...

Harvard Joe & The Fisherman (adapted with permission from Dr. Mark Albion's *The Good Life*)

After graduating from Harvard Business School and working around the clock for years, a stock broker named Joe took a vacation. He chose a small island, famous for its quiet fishing village and local smiles. To take his mind off work, Joe vowed he would avoid the money-talk so prevalent on Wall Street.

On his first vacation day, Joe strolled along the beach and spotted a small boat coming into shore. Inside the boat were a lone fisherman and a fresh catch of large yellow-fin tunas. Dozens of tourists were handing over cash as the fisherman docked his boat. Joe was so impressed, he asked how long it took to fetch such a large bounty of fish ...

FISHERMAN: "I catch plenty within a few hours. The supply is endless here."

JOE: "It's only 9:00 a.m.! You could make a lot more money in such rich waters." What do you do with the rest of your day?"

FISHERMAN: "I read to my kids, practice yoga, and feed the poor. In the afternoons, I walk to the village where I sip wine with my wife and play guitar with friends. Most nights we cook fish and share recipes with tourists."

JOE: "Wow! You have tons of free time! If you'll indulge me, I can help expand your business. I have a Harvard MBA, and it occurs to me that if you simply spent more time fishing, you could earn enough money to run a fleet of boats, sell directly to retailers, and vastly increase your profits."

FISHERMAN: "That's amazing! Then what?"

JOE: "You could sell to all the local islands, open your own sushi bar, or maybe start a franchise. The possibilities are endless in a treasure trove like this!"

FISHERMAN: "I see. How long would all this take?"

JOE: "Not long. Maybe ten years, but with me as your CEO, I'll bet we can do it in seven. I'm all about the hustle! With the right branding and marketing, we can even sell franchises and you would be a multi-millionaire."

FISHERMAN: "Fascinating! What would I do if I was a millionaire?"

JOE: "Sky's the limit! You could retire ... move to a coastal village ... fish when you like ... play guitar with friends ... cook with your wife and kids ... and ..."

Without another word, the fisherman winked and the two men shared a good laugh. By sunset, the fisherman had built a small fire to share his catch-of-the-day, and Joe enjoyed the most amazing fish he ever tasted. As the sun faded, Joe and the tourists sang along to the acoustic sound of the fisherman's guitar.

"Ahhh," Joe whispered. "The good life."

Essential vs. Non-Essential Money Matters

Money mastery is not the focus of this book, but a healthy *Mindset* about personal finance is just as important as any other success principle. So take a good look at your *Essentials* and *Non-Essentials*, then list everything from fixed costs to impulse spending. Don't forget to add up your daily, monthly, and annual expenses from $5 lattes and $15 cocktails to $100 luxury items and weekend getaways!

There's no denying that most people start with a tight budget, but as a financial consultant, I challenge even my wealthiest clients to "GET REAL" with budget expenses. That means accounting for the obvious and not-so-obvious items *(rent, auto, food, phone, grooming, beauty products, clothes, insurance, health, phones, utilities, wifi, cable, gifts, travel, taxes, kids, pets, luxuries, emergencies).*

Can you work harder or smarter to earn more (salary, commission, overtime)? Did you carefully review all your assets (art, jewelry, real estate, furniture, garage-sale items) in relation to debt balances (loans, credit cards, mortgages). Can something be sold to payoff debt or increase savings? Can you cut back on non-essential expenses or earn an extra $100/week? That's $5,200/per year ($52,000 over 10 years). How about an extra $200/per week? That's $10,400 per year ($104,000 over 10 years)!

GO TO NEXT PAGE for MY BUDGET SHEET

Are spending habits in alignment with your definition of The Good Life? Create separate budgets for personal, business, or special projects.

My Budget

Monthly Income: Salary, Commissions, Interest Dividends, Side Jobs, Gifts, Grants, Family Trust, Other Revenue Sources

Monthly Expenses: Rent, Auto, Food, Phone, Beauty, Clothes, Wifi, Insurance, Health, Utilities, Gifts, Travel, Taxes, Kids, Pets, Emergencies

INCOME	($)	EXPENSES	($)
TOTAL		**TOTAL**	

INCOME	-	EXPENSES	=	CASH FLOW

Mindset 2
Unleash Your Entrepreneurial Soul

"Being realistic is the most common road to mediocrity."
WILL SMITH
Actor, Producer, Entrepreneur

*"Embrace what you don't know, especially in the beginning,
because what you don't know can be your greatest asset."*
SARA BLAKELY
Entrepreneur, Philanthropist

Boldly Go!

FROM CLASSROOM TO BOARDROOM and battlefield to playing field, we all have an entrepreneurial spirit. It's in the artist and athlete as much as the CEO or scientist. It's in every pioneer who boldly goes where others only dream. At their core, entrepreneurs lie awake at night with a driving force that says, "There's a better way." By definition, they are misfits who are willing to fail or be ridiculed for their wild ideas. In those moments of chaos, these so-called *crazy ones* not only make a difference, they unleash their entrepreneurial souls.

A Brief History of Entrepreneurial Thinkers

My innovative mindset began with history books, introducing me to thinkers such as Socrates (469 BC - 399 BC) and Aristotle (384 BC - 322 BC). Greek philosophers were ideal teachers because they asked relentless questions about life and business. In middle school, I was fascinated by the Renaissance Age and Leonardo da Vinci (1452-1519), whose talent as an artist, inventor, and scientist inspired me to learn more from creative people. By the time I was twelve, I began studying Benjamin Franklin (1706-1790), a multi-faceted thinker during the American Enlightenment whose insatiable appetite for knowledge made him an influential writer, activist, inventor, and politician. As my studies reached the 20th century, I discovered the great Thomas Edison (1847-1831). He not only pioneered long-lasting light bulbs, he revolutionized the movie industry, innovation lab, and marketing strategies still used by entrepreneurs today. As a teenager however, I was most heavily influenced by martial-arts master Bruce Lee (1940-1973). As a pioneering actor, filmmaker, athlete, humanitarian, and philosopher of East-West principles, Lee gave us the simplest instructions with the most powerful punch. "Always be yourself" and "Be a practical dreamer backed by action."

I'll touch more on these mentors later, but the core lesson from their wisdom is to constantly ask, "WHAT IF?" and "WHY NOT?"

We All Start as Virgins

Most of you know the story of British billionaire Richard Branson who turned the Virgin moniker into one of the most recognized brands in history. He was neither a privileged child, nor did he finish high school. He battled dyslexia and said it made him a better reader of people and situations. That was an insightful lesson for me because it changed my outlook on how I dealt with my own learning challenges.

In spite of setbacks, Branson's multi-national conglomerate, Virgin Group, boasts hundreds of companies in dozens of countries with over 50,000 employees. This colossal triumph in fields ranging from health and finance to travel and entertainment begs a key question: "Where does an entrepreneurial soul like Branson's really begin?"

Born in 1950, Branson started a magazine at 16 with no formal business training, merely a desire to make his mark on the world. The publication was called *Student*, and the mission was to influence contemporary thinking in the late '60s. At the same time, there was a culture of activism which Branson embraced, and the experience of running a magazine forced him to learn leadership principles. He once said, "I wanted to be a journalist and wasn't interested in being an entrepreneur, but I had to become one to keep my magazine going."

Student Magazine only made a few thousand dollars each year, but it was a stepping stone to Branson's music company, Virgin Records (founded in 1972). The name Virgin was proposed by an employee because Branson (age 22) and his peers were so new to business. Nonetheless, Virgin was fueled by clever use of ad space in the back of *Student Magazine*. In time, Branson opened a retail store, built a studio, and started signing recording artists.

A big part of Virgin's rise in a competitive industry was taking risks. When a new sound called punk hit the scene, Branson was willing to sign controversial artists such as The Sex Pistols. Before the industry realized the changing landscape, Virgin had everyone under contract from Boy George's Culture Club to mega stars like the Rolling Stones and Phil Collins. By the '80s, Virgin was one of the top record labels in the world.

Flying high, Branson launched Virgin Atlantic Airways, but with business struggling in 1992, he had to sell the record label to keep his airline going. It was a challenging time, but EMI Records acquired Virgin Records for a reported one billion dollars. As a result, Branson and Virgin continued to take flight.

By 2010, Branson was as well known for Virgin as he was for daredevil journeys in hot-air balloons. A creative and down-to-earth style connected Branson to customers, employees, and partners. His hippy-like persona and uncanny ability to infuse entrepreneurial spirit within his corporate cultures, empowered others to build creative and collaborative environments. These leadership *Essentials* have made Branson well known for his bottom-up managerial style.

"Let's have fun and provide amazing customer experiences" is far more the Branson mantra than "Let's make money." He's repeatedly said that happiness motivates him more than profits. His most *Essential Mindsets* include creativity and imagination. Focus *Strategies* include innovation and communication with flexible leadership. *Values* include integrity, humility, and gratitude. *Purpose* is centered on family, adventure, health, happiness, and making a difference.

Branson doesn't just talk about mission, vision, and values — he lives them. His philanthropic company, Virgin Unite, includes efforts to protect human rights, support education, and preserve the environment. He's worked with world leaders from Nelson Mandela to music activists like Peter Gabriel. He was even knighted Sir Richard by the Queen of England for his contributions to a generation of entrepreneurs.

As I learned more about Branson's journey, I saw interesting parallels to my own. Like many misfits who start with a virgin mindset, I was just a dropout who wanted to be a writer and shake up the establishment. With each pioneer that I studied, I was empowered with the idea that anyone could create exceptional art, make a difference, or unleash an entrepreneurial soul. Like da Vinci, Edison, or Branson, we simply have to ask "WHAT IF? and WHY NOT?"

Visualize Your Brand

An *Essential* thread to career and business excellence is vision. Brand-conscious entrepreneurs create products, services, and companies that stand the test of time. A perfect example is the work of my favorite modern author, J.K. Rowling, who wrote the *Harry Potter* series. Although Rowling was rejected by a dozen publishers who couldn't see her vision, she wrote fantasy books about universal themes kids and adults could always relate to (good vs. evil and hope vs. despair). As a result, the *Harry Potter* franchise (books & films) will be around for generations of fans who believe in the magic of misfits.

Another personal branding lesson I admire came from actor-comedian Jim Carrey. In 2014, he gave a commencement speech to graduates of Maharishi University. From his trials and triumphs, he inspired students with a multi-faceted message around this theme: "You can fail at what you don't want, so you might as well take a chance at doing what you love." As a road map to the right career, Carrey suggested students ask themselves, "What do people need that my talent can serve?" He then concluded the presentation with this gem, "The effect you have on others is the most valuable currency there is." When I heard the speech, it reminded me of a fun story Carrey tells about his own vision as a starving comedian. He was so dedicated to a career that made people laugh, he wrote himself a check for $10 million dollars before he was famous. Thanks to his lead role in the movie *Dumb & Dumber*, he cashed the check a few years later.

I also learned about future branding from entrepreneurs who set industry standards. Howard Schultz (Starbucks) pictured a coffee-community experience. Bill Gates (Microsoft) and Steve Jobs (Apple) imagined software and personal computers in every home, school, and business. Jeff Bezos (Amazon) had a dream to become the earth's biggest retailer. Walt Disney said, "It's fun to do the impossible!" He then created theme parks beyond imagination (Disneyland).

Before all those modern juggernauts however, one of my favorite entrepreneurs set the bar for time-tested brands back in the '50s. Even Millennials know the TV show *I Love Lucy* (1951-1957), the longest-running syndicated show in history. The comedic brainchild of Lucille Ball and her husband, Desi Arnaz, *I Love Lucy* set the standard for entertainment brands with vision.

Lucy was initially told by drama school teachers that she had no future in entertainment (cue the audience laugh track here). However, from the '30s to the '70s, she was a model, dancer, singer, radio voice, theater performer, TV star, film actress, and arguably the greatest female comedian in history. She not only had one of the longest careers in Hollywood, but was the first woman to head a major studio (Desilu).

Lucy and Desi not only had the foresight to create their own production company, they retained ownership and distribution rights of their intellectual property, including *I Love Lucy*. They also knew the quality of old-school film reels wouldn't stand the test of time on television, so they became the first TV producers to use multiple camera angles and motion-picture film in front of a live audience. Desilu even produced some of the most watched shows in history which later became blockbuster movies, such as *Star Trek* and *Mission Impossible*.

Although Desi was half the talent and a maverick in his own right, it was Lucy who broke new ground in a male-dominated profession at a time when it was neither fashionable nor politically correct. She also shattered the glass ceiling for a future generation of pioneering women in entertainment such as Carol Burnett and Mary Tyler Moore in the '70s, and modern icons like Queen Latifah, Jennifer Lopez, Tina Fey, and Ellen DeGeneres. With millions of fans worldwide, each of these women became trusted brands for equality, giving back, business excellence, and personal empowerment.

The Oprah Effect on Learning & Branding

The bar was obviously set in the '90s by Oprah Winfrey. Born in Mississippi (1954), her journey from extreme poverty to a global brand is a tribute to the entrepreneurial mindset. She not only became the world's first African-American woman to hit billionaire status, but a game-changing educator with a genuine love for learning. At a time when book sales were on the decline and reality TV was on the rise, Oprah did something unheard of for a talk-show host. She launched *Oprah's Book Club* in 1996, reminding millions of viewers to embrace literature. From classic fiction to self-help advice, Oprah's influence became so relevant that if she introduced a book it became a bestseller. This marketing bonanza became known as *The Oprah Effect*.

In spite of a childhood that began with abuse, Oprah says she was blessed to have a grandmother who taught her to read at age three. She ended up skipping two early grades and became an honor student. After winning an oratory contest, she earned a full scholarship to Tennessee State University where she studied communication. She then worked at a local radio station during college years and became the youngest female news anchor at Nashville's WLAC-TV. By 1983, she landed a gig hosting *AM Chicago*, a poorly-rated TV talk show, but Oprah catapulted the show from last place to #1 in America (surpassing daytime-TV pioneer Phil Donahue).

Oprah was able to change the talk-show landscape by relating to people on a personal level through her own vulnerability. That authentic style connected with a mass audience in a way that was uncommon at the time. She also understood the power of social media long before Facebook and Twitter. Her passion for self-discovery and accountability raised the bar for students, teachers, parents, and entrepreneurs, not just television ratings.

During her unprecedented talk-show run of 25 years, Oprah launched *O Magazine*, the *Oprah Winfrey Network*, and *Oprah's Angel Network*. Shes's raised a fortune for charities, and even created her own Leadership Academy in South Africa for underprivileged girls. Between talk shows and philanthropy, Oprah also starred in several Oscar-winning films such as *The Butler* and *The Color Purple*. For Oprah, a focus on education, empowerment, and entrepreneurship, not only fulfilled her purpose, but provided a path for millions to do the same.

Study Your Favorite Entrepreneurs

You've now met a few of my favorite mentors. With books, movies, and the Internet, you can study anyone that helps unleash your entrepreneurial soul. Just have the audacity to ask "WHAT IF?" For naysayers who question your total lack of common sense, simply reply, "WHY NOT?"

Thomas Edison

Benjamin Franklin

Bruce Lee

Richard Branson

J.K. Rowling

Jim Carrey

Lucille Ball

Oprah Winfrey

Mindset 3
Cultivate a Creative Mindset

> *"You can't depend on your eyes*
> *when your imagination is out of focus."*
> MARK TWAIN
> Author, Humorist
>
> *"If you're not prepared to be wrong,*
> *you'll never come up with anything original."*
> SIR KEN ROBINSON
> Author, Speaker, Education Activist

The Paradigm Shift in Classrooms & Workplaces

Education activist and creativity expert Sir Ken Robinson is famous for an inspirational Ted Talk he gave in 2006 that's been viewed over 40 million times (*Do Schools Kill Creativity*). It illustrates how we've stigmatized kids who don't excel at a specific curriculum or grading system, and failed to provide environments for the thing they actually love (such as music, dance, or the arts). To illustrate the point, Robinson tells a funny story about a little girl who is told she didn't understand her school assignment. The teacher asked her what she was drawing. The girl replied, "God." The teacher said, "No one knows what God looks like." The little girl then said, "They will in a minute when I'm done drawing this picture."

The joke isn't just an indictment of the teacher who failed to acknowledge the girl's potential as an artist — it's indicative of a stoic education program. The days of teaching static, industrial-style content without acknowledging unique student abilities makes no sense. Education, business, and government institutions who fail to provide experiential, peer-to-peer learning have already fallen behind the curve (socially, academically, and economically). Paradigm shifts are gathering force in classrooms and workplaces around the globe. It's not a matter of when — it's a matter of which teachers and innovators will drive the revolution.

Focus On Your Best Learning Style

The best way I can explain my particular reading challenge is to imagine some-one shaking up your etch-a-sketch while you're still drawing. As for math, the number 6 sometimes looks like a 9. I'm also highly visual and verbal, but that's not always ideal when my creative side wants to battle my logical side. It's quite a party and I'm not sure how everyone got invited!

In my late twenties however, my father (a psychiatrist) suggested I read a few books on "secrets of the brain" and "unique learning styles." The blended study of neurology and psychology not only helped me better understand my learning strengths and weaknesses, I gained an appreciation for the unique style of others. In that "aha" moment, I realized that embracing the talent of other people can shore up our own weaknesses.

Artists and photographers learn best through visual means. Philosophers and psychologists learn best through listening, discussion, and self-reflection. Leaders, salespeople, and politicians learn best through verbal and social in-teraction. Authors, lawyers, and journalists are more proficient with written or spoken words. Scientists, engineers, and economists analyze the world through logic and math. Singers, musicians, and composers are more in tune to music, rhythm, and sound. Environmentalists connect best with nature and their sur-roundings. Kinesthetic learners develop insight through physical movement, such as athletes, dancers, and yogis. In short, we all have unique learning abilities. Some are stronger by nature, while others must be nurtured.

Conceived in 1983, early credit in the study of different learning abilities goes to Harvard psychology professor, Dr. Howard Gardner. In his book, *Frames of Mind: The Theory of Multiple Intelligences,* Gardner suggested that traditional ways of measuring intelligence are too limiting, such as I.Q. Testing. So he proposed a modern idea which outlined our unique thinking styles. Gardner's theories are well described in two of my favorite books, *Emotional Intelligence (1995 & 2006)* and *Social Intelligence (2006),* both written by another Harvard psychology professor, Dr. Daniel Goleman. The real-world lessons in these books provide terrific road maps to how we think, learn, and grow.

Social & Emotional Intelligence are defined as follows ... ➤

1 Emotional Intelligence
Our self-awareness, self-discipline, and ability to manage emotions. This is a basic understanding of **what drives me.**

2 Social Intelligence
Our ability to empathize, get along, and read situations. This is a basic understanding of **what drives other people**.

Insight to our intelligence styles enables us to see how strength or weakness in one skill can dramatically impact another. For example, what good is emotional intelligence (self-awareness) without social intelligence (empathy for others)? In *The 4 Essentials*, what good is a creative or positive mindset without strategies, values, and purpose? When we understand our best learning styles, we can also fill gaps by collaborating with those who have abilities different yet complimentary to our own.

The brain is also a muscle, so each intelligence style gets stronger with practice. If we fail to stretch our verbal and listening skills, emotional and social intelligence will suffer. By the same token, if you practice piano and read music, you might fire up your math and reasoning skills. With so many learning styles, there's no need to be frustrated if you don't master them all, because no one ever does. The trick is to focus on strengths and what you love, then delegate and collaborate your weak points. Simply ask, "Where can I bridge gaps between what I don't know, don't do well, or don't enjoy?" These are *Essential* exercises for students, leaders, teachers, and entrepreneurs alike.

Intelligence Styles		Definition of Styles
1 EMOTIONAL	»	SELF-AWARE & SELF-REFLECTIVE
2 SOCIAL	»	EMPATHETIC WITH PEOPLE SKILLS
3 VERBAL	»	SPEAKING & WRITING SKILLS
4 VISUAL	»	SPATIAL AWARENESS OF OBJECTS
5 LOGICAL	»	INTUITIVE WITH NUMBERS & PATTERNS
6 TACTILE	»	IN TOUCH WITH BODY & MOVEMENT
7 MUSICAL	»	IN TUNE WITH SOUND & RHYTHMS
8 NATURALISTIC	»	IN TOUCH WITH SURROUNDINGS

No one is limited by a learning challenge or style preference. A shy entrepreneur can partner with a socially savvy salesperson. A doctor with poor people skills can learn to be more empathetic by hiring a caring staff. A world-class athlete may not be tech-savvy, but he can always add a computer buddy to his network. In short, our personal and professional networks should always be growing. With a little luck, social and emotional intelligence might even rub off, not merely fill our gaps.

Unlock Your Inner Da Vinci

Shortly after college, I was sitting in a café with a few pals, chatting about Leonardo da Vinci. My friends talked for hours about creative principles that could be learned by studying one of the great Renaissance minds who transcended art, science, and engineering. At one point I said, "I doubt any of us will paint The Mona Lisa simply by studying da Vinci." My friends laughed at me for being so shortsighted, and for the next three hours I got slammed for my ignorance.

My friends explained that da Vinci actually had an *Essential* system that nourished his passion for work, play, and innovation. His principles have been widely adopted by individuals and corporations for centuries. Often known as a man of mystery (dramatized in Dan Brown's *The Da Vinci Code*), there were thousands of pages in da Vinci's notebooks that provide insight to his creative process. It's a similar system that many educators try to replicate in the best schools and corporate training programs worldwide. To my pleasant surprise, the da Vinci formula features primary tenets of *The 4 Essentials* (alignment of mindset, strategies, values, and purpose).

Published 165 years after his death in 1684, da Vinci's journals reveal that he scribbled notes and drawings every day. From humor, art, music, and culture to science, medicine, and inventions, he had a system for connecting everything he saw. Many historians say his notes were so random they lacked coherence, but to artists and innovators that was his genius.

Although da Vinci may have been blessed with a creative spark at birth that many of us were not, he was also considered attention deficit because he failed to finish many projects that he started. When entrepreneurs study this all-to-familiar story, they discover that da Vinci compensated for his shortcomings through creative routines. Similarly, if our goal is to transform classrooms, boardrooms, and workplaces for the 21st century, it's imperative that we cultivate creative-thinking environments for students, leaders, teachers, and professionals alike.

Even billionaire Bill Gates paid $30 million dollars in 1994 to study one of da Vinci's notebooks called *The Codex Leicester* (now on display in different cities). The price tag makes it the most valuable manuscript in the world. In reviewing the 500-year-old journal, Gates said, "It's an inspiration that da Vinci, without being told what was right or wrong, kept pushing himself, and found knowledge itself to be the most beautiful thing."

---

5 Steps to a Da Vinci Mindset

Creative Step 1: Always be curious
Maintain an insatiable passion about people, places, and things.

Creative Step 2: Dream it • Discuss it • Do it
Visualize, talk about your ideas, and put words into action.

Creative Step 3: Surround yourself with talent
Get others involved to help you think outside the box.

Creative Step 4: Maintain a daily journal
Jot down highlights of what you see, think, and hear each day.

Creative Step 5: See problems as possibilities
Unchain your mind with creative solutions and no boundaries.

Creative Underdogs & Underwater Dreams

When my pal Mary Mazzio (an award-winning filmmaker) released her latest documentary about underdogs, I was excited to share it with the world. Launched in late 2014, Mazzio produced *Underwater Dreams* with a grass roots movement. What happened within two years was nothing short of the miracle depicted in her film.

Narrated by actor Michael Peña, *Underwater Dreams* is the epic, true story of undocumented Mexican-immigrant students who battled the best minds from MIT and other colleges in an underwater robotics competition, sponsored by NASA and the Navy. Inspired by their two science teachers, Fredi Lajvardi and Allan Cameron, four kids at Arizona's Carl Hayden High School signed up for the robotics team. Like many immigrants, these kids came to America in the back of trucks with nothing but dreams of a better life. Little did they know they were about to play David to MIT's Goliath in the summer of 2004.

With an initial goal to simply have a great learning experience, the rag-tag team of Oscar Vazquez, Lorenzo Santillan, Cristian Arcega, and Luis Aranda called ocean engineers and military contractors for help. They had just four months to raise money and build an underwater robot. They got local businesses to donate $800 for critical parts, but all they could afford was PVC pipe and duct tape from Home Depot. Nonetheless, they built a robot and named it Stinky (thanks to the smell of rubber glue that held it together).

Hoping not to finish last, the students piled into a beat-up van and headed to the California competition at UC Santa Barbara. The boys walked into the contest area overwhelmed by college teams dressed in matching gear, showing off robots sponsored by the likes of Exxon Mobil. When it was time to put Stinky in the water for a test run, the robot leaked. Each team had only 12 hours to fix their issues, so one of the Carl Hayden kids suggested plugging the leak with a Super-Plus tampon — and it worked! Against all odds, they went on to beat the best brains from MIT and other college elites.

It's important to note that Mazzio's film was funded and supported not only by republican and democratic leaders like President Barack Obama, Jeb Bush, and Joe Kennedy, but powerhouse organizations like Babson College, the Bezos Foundation, and the Laurie M. Tisch Illumination Fund.

Shortly after the movie launch, there was a nationwide buzz about STEM education reform (Science, Technology, Engineering, Math). As political and academic worlds collided, Mazzio found herself screening the film at both the White House and The Clinton Global Initiative. Soon after, Mazzio and the Carl Hayden team embarked on a 100-city movie tour in partnership with AMC Theaters, where schools and non-profits were encouraged to see the film for free!

Underwater Dreams was so inspiring that leaders in politics, business, and academics began discussing immigration and education reform in a whole new light. Along the way, the "Let Everyone Dream Coalition" was founded in response to President Obama's charge to find creative ways to support STEM education. MIT and major donors were so affected by the story, it united corporate investors, universities, and non-profits to increase STEM education for under-represented students. As of 2016, the coalition had raised over $100 million dollars. With over $20 million dedicated to the Coalition in 2015, Wellesley College in particular has been a leader in STEM education for women. The whole story just goes to show, even creative underdogs can do the impossible!

*NOTE: The story of the Carl Hayden Robotics team also became a major motion picture.

(Spare Parts, a Lionsgate Film • 2015)

Mindset 4
Build a Result-Driven Practice

"I'm convinced that half of what separates successful entrepreneurs from non-successful ones is pure perseverance."
STEVE JOBS
Co-Founder, Apple Computers

In Search of Excellence

IN HIS BEST-SELLING BOOK *Outliers,* Malcolm Gladwell provides insightful stories to reinforce a simple theory: that **focus, opportunity,** and **experience** are keys to success. Gladwell also suggests that being really great at something like math, sports, or music, usually requires **10 years** or **10,000 hours** of **practice**.

I once thought practice made perfect too, until I took up golf in my twenties and seriously questioned *The Outlier Theory.* No matter how hard I practiced my insane slice, I still ended up in the woods (even with expert coaching). My weekend golf pals got even worse with time — disturbingly worse! So if focus, opportunity, and 10,000 hours of experience aren't the answer, what are the common threads to peak performance? With 25 years of personal research, I discovered that excellence (by any definition) is far more dependent on **result-driven practice with purpose** than anything else.

Let's examine a few outliers ...

Result-Driven Practice with Passion & Purpose

There are people who have innate skills, specialized training, and a competitive edge (eg: musical composers, logical engineers, kinesthetic athletes). However, talent, supportive coaches, and practice alone aren't proxies for success. Since there are gifted, hard-working people who accomplish little, we have to ask, "What's the most proven formula for successful students, athletes, and innovators?"

Most of us show up and work hard every day. Some people improve and others don't. This is why the old cliché *"practice makes perfect"* is somewhat misguided. You can practice the same skill for 20 years and perform no better in year 21 than day one. *The key to measurable success is a result-driven routine with an inspirational mission behind your practice.* This is as true for the Sunday golfer or piano prodigy, as it is for the software developer or game-changing CEO.

Wolfgang Mozart & Tiger Woods

To illustrate my theory on practice principles, let's first examine a few outliers such as composer Wolfgang "Amadeus" Mozart and golfer Eldrick "Tiger" Woods. Wolfgang's father (Leopold Mozart) had a love for music composition. Tiger's father (Earl Woods) had a deep passion for golf. Each parent created an early opportunity for his kid to grow into a skill that the father first mastered to a high degree. Both parents also decided that their kids were special at birth and mapped a course for greatness (music for Wolfgang and golf for Tiger). In other words, the kids received expert, around-the-clock coaching, under the watchful eye of emotionally-vested fathers (some would say obsessed, so these weren't normal circumstances). It's not to say Mozart and Woods didn't have natural talent, but were they born prodigies as we've been led to believe?

Wolfgang's father was a public composer and disciplinarian who wrote a modern handbook for the violin. He began teaching piano to Wolfgang at age 3. Historians tell us his father also had him composing by age 5 and performing publicly at age 8. However, there are no compositions in pre-school Wolfgang's handwriting. This suggests early work may have been written (or at least corrected in part) by his father. Wolfgang's earliest compositions as a schoolboy also sounded quite familiar to his contemporaries. In today's music world, this might be considered "sampling a competitor's work" to create a popular song.

I'm not suggesting we minimize the greatness of Mozart's music, nor implying he lifted a few good tunes, but the notion that he began composing masterpieces out of whole cloth (or divine spark) as a gifted preschooler is worth debating. According to classical experts, Mozart's greatest achievements occurred between ages 21 and 35. This means he didn't hit full stride until after 18 to 30 years of hyper-focused work. This is blasphemy to Mozart lovers who buy the outlier theory, but fascinating if we're having an honest dialogue about whether a genius is born or meticulously developed.

In the sports world, Tiger Woods is considered an athletic genius. In reality, he's Mozart on the golf course. Similar to Wolfgang's father, Tiger's dad (Earl Woods) loved to teach. He began grooming his son for greatness as soon as he could hold a mini-golf club at age 2. Earl Woods then took Tiger on a TV show to show off the "natural swing" of his prodigy, but there's much more to the story.

Tiger's dad was a United States Army Green Beret (retired). Like Mozart's father, Earl Woods taught intensive work regimens to his son, starting with professional golf lessons at age 4. This result-driven practice had a singular purpose — to create the greatest golfer of all time. To no one's surprise, Tiger turned pro straight out of college and eclipsed nearly every record in golf history. By 2009 (age 33), he won 14 Major Championships (2nd best all time) and 71 Professional Tournaments (3rd best all time). By 2010, he racked up $1 billion dollars in tour and endorsement earnings, and was the youngest player to win a Grand Slam (*The Masters, U.S. Open, British Open, PGA Championship*).

Does anyone still believe Tiger's "outlier" accomplishments are the mere result of good genes, practice time, and experience? Of course not. Tiger credits his father for teaching him purpose-driven routines that had military precision (even under extreme pressure). Case in point: Tiger can stop a golf swing when an unexpected roar erupts from a crowd just as he's about to strike the ball. This is extraordinarily difficult, but an Earl Woods "coaching session" included screaming and dropping golf bags during practice swings. This enabled Tiger to block out even the most startling distractions. How many other professional golfers developed a military mindset under the discerning eye of an Army Green Beret since childhood? Zero. Hence, the outlier.

Without a doubt, Mozart was naturally musical which means he may have been an equally-talented painter or mathematician. Woods is kinesthetic which means his hand-eye coordination could have made him world-class in many sports. Those musical and athletic traits were essential to Mozart and Woods, but their innate abilities did not ensure success. Upon close examination, we discover that most of their achievements were actually based on *result-driven practice with passion and purpose.**

*NOTE: In 2009, Tiger Woods displayed many gaps in his *Life Essentials*, highlighted by a lack of integrity and weak emotional intelligence. These flaws culminated in a breach of public and private trust that severely interrupted his career momentum. He stated unequivocally that "Becoming a better human being would be the key to future success."

Steve Jobs & Bill Gates

Most people know the stories of Microsoft pioneer Bill Gates and Apple vision-ary Steve Jobs. They're two of the most recognized figures in history. Volumes have been written about both computer giants so I can't offer much to their biographies. However, there's an interesting lesson I picked up watching one of the 2010 Apple commercials comparing PC to Mac.

In a cheeky ad campaign, Apple enjoys poking fun at Microsoft's history of software problems. It's not as if Apple never had to make improvements too, but since the PC is known to crash more often than the Mac, the audience gets the joke. The campaign was clever marketing, but I came away with a totally different take than the one Apple intended. In the commercial, a hip-looking kid in jeans (symbolic of Steve Jobs) stands next to an older-looking nerd who is wearing a suit and glasses (symbolic of Bill Gates). The dialogue goes like this:

KID MAC: "Hello, I'm a Mac."

PC GATES (SMILING): "And I'm a PC. Hey Mac, did you hear the good news? Windows 7 is out and it's not going to have any of the problems that my last operating system had. Trust me."

KID MAC (SUSPICIOUSLY): "I feel like I've heard this before, PC."

For the next 60 seconds, we see PC Gates in goofy leisure suits from the '80s, insisting that each new version of Microsoft will be better than the prior ones.

PC GATES (STILL SMILING & WINKING): "Windows Vista is here and it won't have any of the problems Windows '98 had ... or Windows '95 ... or Windows 2. This time it's gonna be different. Trust me."

What I gleaned from this little history lesson wasn't that Mac was better than PC, or Apple better than Microsoft, or Jobs better than Gates. There are pros and cons to both. My take was that Gates and Jobs never stopped innovating. Microsoft was still working out the kinks on *Windows 7.0* when I wrote this book in 2012. By the time I wrote the second edition in 2016, Microsoft had released *Windows 10.0* and a whole new line of modern laptops.

In spite of glitch after glitch, Gates dominated the software industry for de-cades through *result-driven innovation*. Similarly, Jobs took us through multiple technology revolutions with a vision for every Apple product to be "insanely great!" After all, he was never satisfied with his first home computers. Apple Lisa, Apple II, and Macintosh were heavily-flawed machines. Jobs also demanded annual, result-driven improvements to the user experience of iPods, iPads, iPhones and iTunes. By the time you finish reading this chapter, new versions of every Apple product will be on display — TRUST ME!

Although Steve Jobs passed away in 2011, his core lesson lives on: "Don't just think different. Be different." This classic mantra reminds us that we don't admire Gates and Jobs just because they had pioneering ideas. By all counts, they were very flawed human beings (even tyrants in their early years) who often treated employees with disdain. They wanted so badly to lead their industry that their social and emotional integrity left much to be desired (Mozart and Woods suffered from the same shortcomings). What's admirable about Jobs and Gates as entrepreneurs however is that they never stopped asking, "How can I make the customer experience better?" For any of us to harness the same practice strategies, we can't rest on past performance. If the goal is to be "insanely great," then the best outlier formula is to ask: "WHAT'S NEXT?"

Your Peak Performance Playbook

Everyone has potential greatness in their DNA, regardless of their challenges. Consider Stevie Wonder, Ray Charles, and Andrea Bocelli. Each of these multi-talented singers is blind, but also a Grammy award-winning recording artist who developed timeless music and vocal abilities through relentless work and vision.

How about Queen Latifah, Jennifer Lopez, Michael Jackson or The Beatles? Was it privilege, or did they all rise to the top of their field through a *hard day's night, workin' like a dog, eight days a week*? We find the same *Essentials* practiced by legendary martial arts master Bruce Lee, baseball pioneer Jackie Robinson, tennis stars Serena and Venus Williams, and countless others.

As for you, me, and Average Joe, the nurture-versus-nature debate ended long ago. Brains, opportunity, and raw talent are never enough. There's a quality of persistence and sacrifice that separates world-class athletes, musicians, and entrepreneurs from mere players and pretenders. In fact, the *Outlier Theory* which requires ten thousand hours for success doesn't apply at all to those who must focus on short-term projects. Sorry, Malcolm!

> The secret to peak performance has always been result-driven practice with passion, purpose & persistence.

Mindset 5
Show Grit & Never Quit

> *"There's a way to do it better — find it. Show me a*
> *thoroughly satisfied man and I'll show you a failure."*
> THOMAS EDISON
> Inventor, Scientist, Entrepreneur

My Failure Philosophy

I BEGAN A VIGOROUS study of success principles at 17, but it wasn't long before I realized that most people didn't achieve breakthroughs without battle scars (especially innovators). My failures as a young entrepreneur were no exception, so I appreciated early in life that there was a big difference between losing and those who learn from defeat. To that end, I cultivated an *Essential* life philosophy from two historical mentors: Thomas Edison and Abraham Lincoln. A brief study of their mental discipline is a lesson that's hard to forget ...

Edison's Secret to Innovation

My first role model on how to learn from failure was Thomas Edison. Among his pioneering inventions, he launched the multi-billion-dollar era of industrial labs, sound recordings, motion pictures, and long-lasting light bulbs. He also raised the bar for market-testing strategies that modern entrepreneurs still use today, making his uncommon journey and mental mindset worth learning.

Edison was the youngest of seven children and didn't speak until he was almost four. When he did, he was a hyper and inquisitive kid that a teacher described as "too stupid to learn." As a result, Edison's mother opted for home-schooling. Among his challenges, Edison was technically deaf by his teenage years. In spite of the impairment, he intuitively placed a piece of wood between his teeth to pick up sound vibrations during experiments. The result was ground-breaking research and his invention of the phonograph. Then in 1888, Edison announced a plan to invent "an instrument which does for the eye what the phonograph does for the ear — the recording and reproduction of things in motion." By 1900, the Edison Manufacturing Company became a major producer of motion picture equipment and films.

Known as the "Wizard of Menlo Park" in New Jersey, Edison was much more than an inventor — he was a 20th century entrepreneur, branding expert, and marketing pioneer who started over 100 companies, including General Electric. In fact, he was awarded the first of more than a thousand patents when he was just 22. How did he do so much with supposed hearing and learning challenges? Although his most famous competitor Nicolas Tesla invented the light bulb, it had no practical utility at the time. It was Edison who pioneered a market-ready solution — the long-lasting light bulb. In that simple *battle of the bulb*, we discover why Edison succeeded where Tesla and others didn't? Edison was willing to fail until design ideas actually solved a consumer need and had a bonafide marketing plan. He famously said, "I haven't failed a thousand times, I've successfully found a thousand ways that won't work."

From his factory of workers, countless notebooks reveal thousands of failed prototypes and business theories. The Edison journals indicate that he not only doodled, but far more obsessed with progress than perfection. From his lab, we also find a detailed process that takes full advantage of how to start smart and learn from failed experiments. The Edison Innovation System included:

1) Identifying a clear need
2) The assignment of teams
3) A rigorous process to build prototypes
4) An understanding of consumer reaction
5) A pursuit of the smartest way to service, manufacture, and market the best version of an idea, not just the initial concept

One of the fascinating footnotes to Edison's legacy occurred in 1914, when a chemical explosion destroyed half of his New Jersey factory. He calmly responded, "It's all right, you'll never see a more beautiful fire, and we just destroyed a lot of rubbish. Although I'm 67, I'll start over tomorrow." In short, Edison had a grittier mindset than most of his contemporaries. We see the same principles taught in the most pioneering schools and companies today. We'll discuss more about personal power systems that help overcome adversity in *Essential 2 (Strategies),* and *Essential 4 (Purpose),* but for now, trust the Edison mindset that says, "Failure is your friend!"

Abraham's Arduous Road

"The probability that we may fail shouldn't deter us
from the support of a cause we believe to be just."
ABRAHAM LINCOLN
16th President of the United States

My first year in college, I read a book titled *Decision in Philadelphia*. It's an insightful, true story that captures the triumphs and failures of the Constitutional Convention in 1787. Based in part on session notes by Benjamin Franklin, the book depicts not only the painstaking process of writing the United States Constitution, but the many shortcomings of America's Founding Fathers. These pioneers who wrote so eloquently that "all men are created equal," failed to abolish slavery or provide for women's rights. For a country that was supposed to be grounded in freedom, the failure to ensure basic rights and dignity to all citizens would lead to civil war three-quarters of a century later.

To begin the remedy of this American tragedy, it took a man who not only understood adversity, but had the ability to overcome it, Abraham Lincoln. We know him as the 16th President of the United States and a leader who set the wheels in motion to abolish slavery in the midst of civil war. Historians remind us however that Lincoln's personal character in the face of extraordinary circumstances is what made him such an admirable figure.

In 1809, Lincoln was born to humble and tragic beginnings. His parents were uneducated farmers and his father was illiterate. At age 7, Lincoln's family was forced from their home, his mother died when he was 9 years old, and his only sister died in childbirth when he was 11. His grandfather was killed when Lincoln was 23.

Lincoln is one of ten U.S. Presidents who never graduated from college. At 24, he failed in business and went bankrupt, but he spent the next 17 years paying of debts to friends and colleagues. In spite of the setback, he studied law on his own and became an attorney with an impeccable reputation. Nicknamed "Honest Abe," Lincoln even encouraged clients to avoid litigation if he believed they might experience financial hardship.

At 26, he was engaged to be married, but his fiancé died. A broken-hearted Lincoln had a nervous breakdown and battled depression for some time. At 33, he was married to Mary Todd. They had four sons, but three of them died at ages 4, 11, and 18. This was not uncommon in the nineteenth century when children died of illnesses we could easily treat today.

Lincoln's professional career was equally turbulent. In his mid-20s, he was twice defeated in a run for state legislature. At 29, he picked himself up from personal depression to run for speaker of the state legislature. He was defeated. Although finally elected to the state legislature, Lincoln was defeated several times running for Congress. At 45, he ran for Senate and lost. At 47, he ran for vice president and lost. At 49, he ran for Senate and lost ... again!

In spite of all the setbacks, Lincoln pressed on. Then in 1860, he ran for president (age 50) at the dawn of Civil War, won the election, and changed the course of history. Today, he is probably the most quoted and revered of U.S. Presidents, and one of the most studied leaders of all time. He is also remembered fondly as a statesman of impeccable character, who had so much more to teach, if not for being assassinated in 1865. No doubt, Lincoln's arduous road to the White House reminds us of his most enduring lesson ...

Show grit and never quit!

How to Break a Mental Barrier

I'm claustrophobic, so confined spaces or being underwater scare the hell out of me. Consequently, I nearly missed one of the most rewarding experiences of my life. In 2003, I took a trip with friends to the Great Barrier Reef in Australia. I wanted to overcome two of my greatest fears (sharks and scuba diving).

A few months earlier, I had taken scuba lessons in a swimming pool, but that did nothing to calm my nerves. The minute I stepped on our chartered boat in Australia, I started hyper-ventilating and told everyone it was probably best if I just snorkeled. Fortunately, my friends didn't let me off that easily.

The dive master had similar phobias when he was a boy, so he shared a few lessons about how to break mental barriers. "Cliff, I hear you like yoga, so close your eyes and think of diving as a form of meditation. Imagine being in total harmony with your best friends in a safe place. Breathe deep ... hold it ... now open your eyes." He then played an amazing video of the underwater reef with scuba divers holding hands as they gazed upon a rainbow of fish dancing with sharks. Classical music accompanied the video as I watched in fascination. What the dive master did brilliantly was shift my focus from something mysterious to something beautiful. My only prior memory of a shark was from the movie *JAWS!*

A few hours later, we jumped in the water and my pals formed a circle of trust around me. Holding hands, we submerged a few feet at a time to the ocean floor. I saw colors and creatures I never fathomed, was feeding giant cod fish by hand, and came eye-to-eye with friendly sharks and sea turtles. From that day forward, I've always told friends that self discovery is like scuba diving. We can peek a few feet below the surface or explore a deeper world filled with insight and imagination.

Whatever your great barrier is,
test the waters, then leap and go deep!

The Adversity Hall of Fame

"I don't want to be remembered as the girl who got shot.
I want to be remembered as the girl who stood up."
Malala Yousafzai
Education Activist, Nobel Prize Winner

"I've missed more than 9,000 shots in my career. I've lost
almost 300 games. On 26 occasions, I was entrusted to
take the game-winning shot ... and missed. I've failed over
and over in my life ... and that's why I succeed."
Michael Jordan
Champion Basketball Player

Who	Adversity	Success
Muhammad Ali Boxer, Humanitarian	Stripped of Championship Title & boxing license in prime of career due to his refusal to fight in the Vietnam War. Ridiculed by government & public.	Recaptured Championship. Became one of the most beloved humanitarians & legendary athletes in the world.
Malala Yousafzai Education Activist	Shot in the head by the Taliban when she was just 15 years old.	Became the youngest-ever Nobel Prize laureate and a global inspiration for educating women.
Michael Jordan Basketball Player	Didn't make high-school varsity team as a sophomore – told he was too short.	6-Time NBA Champion. 6-Time League MVP. 2-Time Olympic Gold Medalist.
Wilma Rudolph Track & Field Athlete	She was the 20th of 22 children. She suffered from polio at age 4 and was told she'd never walk. She wore leg braces and walked again by age 12.	At age 16, won an Olympic bronze team track medal. At age 20 (1960 Rome Olympics), she became the first woman to win 3 Gold Medals at the Olympics.
Albert Einstein Theoretical Physicist	Didn't speak until 4 or read until 7. Described by teachers & parents as slow. Expelled from school.	Discovered Theory of Relativity. Synonymous with genius.
Thomas Edison Inventor	Didn't speak until 4, described by teachers as slow, and had a hearing challenge.	Founder of 14 companies, . Owned over a 1000 patents. Inventor of phonograph & long-lasting light bulbs.
Walt Disney Founder, Disney	Fired by news editor for lack of imagination. Went bankrupt. His theme park was initially rejected by the city of Anaheim.	Disney became a pioneer in entertainment & one of the most enduring brands in history.

The Adversity Hall of Fame (continued)

Who	Adversity	Success
Fred Astaire Actor, Singer, Dancer	First screen test 1933 – Director's memo: "Can't act. Can't sing. Slightly bald. Can dance a little."	76-year career. 31 musical films. Considered the greatest dancer in history.
Lucille Ball Comedian, Actress	Considered B-List failure in film. Told by drama teachers she had no future in entertainment.	4-Time Emmy winner. Pioneering TV executive. Greatest female comedian.
The Beatles Rock 'n' roll Band	Rejected by Decca Records. Told, "We don't like their sound. Groups with guitars are on their way out."	Rock 'n' roll Hall of Fame. Top-selling band of all time.
Charlie Chaplin Director, Actor, Comedian	Rejected by movie studios. Told his pantomime was nonsense.	Pioneered silent film era. Co-Founder of United Artists.
Harland Sanders Founder, KFC	At 65, was rejected over 1000 times trying to sell chicken recipe.	KFC became one of the most successful food brands and franchises in history.
Winston Churchill British Leader & Orator	Failed 6th grade. Twice failed entrance exam to military academy. Defeated in political races his entire life until age 62.	Prime Minister of England. Nobel Prize in Literature.
Abraham Lincoln Lawyer, Politician	Born into poverty. Haunted by personal tragedies. Defeated for Congress and Vice President.	16th President of United States. Led country through Civil War. Statesmen, civil rights leader.
Charles M. Schulz Cartoonist	His cartoons were rejected by his high school yearbook and he was rejected for a job with Disney.	Creator of *Peanuts* (Charlie Brown), one of the most enduring cartoons of all time.
Jerry Seinfeld Comedian	First time on stage at a comedy club, he froze and was booed off stage.	Returned next night to applause. His show, *Seinfeld,* ran 9 TV seasons, one of the most successful sitcoms in history.
Steven Spielberg Filmmaker	Rejected 3 times by University of Southern California School of Theater, Film and Television.	Oscar-winning director and producer. His films have grossed $10 billion dollars worldwide.
Oprah Winfrey Talk Show Host, Producer	Born into poverty & experienced a traumatic childhood. Fired from early job as reporter. Told she was "unfit for television."	Oprah's TV show ran 25 years. First African-American, female billionaire & a global brand.

A Special Tribute to Writers

Who	Adversity	Success
J.K. Rowling	Rowling's *Harry Potter* was rejected by 12 publishers.	*Harry Potter* became top-selling book and movie franchise.
Stephen King	First book, *Carrie*, was rejected by publishers 30 times so he threw the manuscript in the garbage.	King's spouse encouraged him to resubmit and *Carrie* was finally published. King went on to sell millions of novels worldwide with many becoming famous movies.
Richard Bach	*Jonathan Livingston Seagull* (*JLS*) was rejected by publishers 18 times.	*JLS* sold millions of copies since its initial publishing in 1972.
Jack Canfield & Mark Victor Hansen	*Chicken Soup for the Soul* was rejected over 30 times in one month and a reported 140 times before publishing.	*Chicken Soup* book franchise sold over 80 million copies, with over 60 subtitles, in over 30 languages.
Margaret Mitchell	*Gone With the Wind* was rejected by publishers 38 times.	Mitchell won a Pulitzer Prize in 1937 and *Gone With the Wind* became a Hollywood treasure.
James Joyce	*Dubliners* was rejected 22 times with only 1,250 copies initially printed and only 379 copies sold in 1914. Joyce is said to have purchased 120 of those.	Joyce became one of the most influential writers of the 20th century. *Dubliners* is a classic collection of his best short stories.
Robert Pirsig	*Zen and the Art of Motorcycle Maintenance* was rejected by publishers 121 times.	The *Zen* classic sold millions of copies after publishing in 1974.
Richard Hornberger	*M*A*S*H* (the novel) was rejected by publishers 21 times.	The book was highly successful and the 1970 Oscar-winning film gave birth to *M*A*S*H*, the longest-running TV series of all time.
Madeleine L'Engle	*A Wrinkle in Time* was rejected by publishers 26 times.	Published in 1962, *A Wrinkle in Time* became one of the best-selling children's books of all time.
Maya Angelou	Born into poverty and an abusive childhood. Was mute for five years after being traumatized.	Award-winning poet, writer, producer with books, plays and movies that spanned 50 years.

Congratulations!

You've just concluded *Essential 1* toward your **Master's** in **Basic Abilities**.

Here's a Recap of Your Top 5 Mindset Essentials

1) Define Success & Happiness

2) Unleash Your Entrepreneurial Soul

3) Cultivate Creative Thinking

4) Build a Result-Driven Practice

5) Show Grit & Never Quit

Essential 2 · **Strategies**

*"Passion, purpose, and principles won't
matter if you're traveling east looking for a sunset."*
Cliff

Align Your Strategies

I N *Essential 1*, I highlighted five critical *Mindsets* for daily practice. In *Essential 2*, I'll introduce five *Strategies* (systems and habits) that will empower any *Mindset*. For example, you may have a positive, creative, or entrepreneurial mindset, but decision-making, leadership, and team-building *Strategies* are equally essential to life, career, and business success.

Master These 5 Strategies to Put Mindset in Motion

1) Take the Self Discovery Path
2) Master Emotional & Communication Intelligence
3) Embrace Chaos, Decisions & Change
4) Work with Teams, Leaders & Mentors
5) Set Goals, Focus & Manage Time

Strategy 1
Take the Self-Discovery Path

"Who in the world am I?
Ah, that's the great puzzle."
LEWIS CAROL
Author (Alice in Wonderland)

Crystallize Your Passion, Purpose & Principles

I N *Essential 1, Mindset 1,* you looked at a few ways to *Define Success and Happiness* by comparing the Wall Street life of a Harvard MBA with an island fisherman. Both are noble pursuits for different people at various stages in life. In this chapter, I'll challenge you to ask self-discovery questions about skills and resources essential to your strategies:

- Why am I doing it?
- What are my unique abilities?
- Do I have the right teammates?
- Are my passions and principles in alignment?

In many cases, self reflection brings up emotions like fear, so it's critical to identify obstacles in order to find the best solutions. Although our intuition is often right, friends and peers will occassionally see things better than we see ourselves. If you're willing to be vulnerable, and answer the hardest questions truthfully, you'll create a faster track to personal and professional growth.

On your path, take a deep breath, trust your gut,
and allow the following parables to serve you well ...

The Greatest Hitter in The World

A young boy from an orphanage approached home plate at an empty baseball field. Alone with his bat and ball, he looked out to center field and shouted, "I'm the greatest home-run hitter in the world!" He tossed the ball in the air, swung and missed. "Strike one," the boy announced to his imaginary fans. He then picked up the ball and shouted even louder, "I'm the greatest home-run hitter in the world!" He tossed the ball in the air, swung, and missed again. "Strike two," he said. Frustrated, the boy pointed his bat to center field with the fierce look of a big-league slugger and shouted with all his might, "I'm the greatest home-run hitter IN THE WORLD!!!" He tossed the ball in the air, swung and missed again. Exhausted, he fell to the ground. "Strike three!" He then smiled and said, "Wow — I must be the greatest pitcher in the world!"

MORAL OF THE STORY
We all strike out on our self-discovery path

The parable above is a true story handed down for generations, but few people realize that it's based on New York Yankee baseball Hall-of-Famer Babe Ruth. Many people forget that he was one of the greatest pitchers of his era and may never have become baseball's home run king if not for a twist of fate.

Initially scouted at St. Mary's Industrial School for Boys in Baltimore, Maryland, Ruth started his career as a pitcher with the Boston Red Sox. He posted phenomenal statistics for four years (18 wins in 1915, 23 wins in 1916 (with 9 shutouts), and 24 wins in 1917). As a pitcher, Ruth even won 3 World Series games without a loss and had 29 scoreless innings. So at one time in history, Babe Ruth truly was "the greatest baseball pitcher in the world."

Then in 1919, Ruth set a Major League record with 29 home runs. With so much focus required for pitching however, he barely scratched the surface of his potential as a hitter. As fate would have it, Boston couldn't afford to pay Ruth as his stock was rising as a slugger, so they traded him to the New York Yankees for $125,000. Sure enough, Ruth became a full-time outfielder the next year, and hit 54 home runs with a menacing .376 batting average. On the road to 714 home runs, a record that lasted half a century, Ruth also struck out 1,330 times. Like the little boy in the baseball parable and all the misfits in this book, Ruth's story reminds us that everyone strikes out on their self-discovery path.

Don't Peter-Principle Yourself

In 1968, a theory was developed by Dr. Laurence Peter called *The Peter Principle*. It explains why promoting someone can backfire if solely based on their experience. In his study, Peter recognized that skills required for a new position were often different than skills required for a prior position. In other words, a worker might get promoted to a level of incompetence that's counterproductive to their passion, purpose, or abilities.

To illustrate, imagine a top car salesman named Jim whose firm promotes him to sales manager and gives him a salary bump with bonus incentives. The promotion requires Jim to manage weekly meetings and twenty salespeople. This sounded great in the beginning, but after six months Jim realized he hated managing salespeople, was neglecting his own clients, and started barking at everyone. The staff loved Jim "the sales guy," but weren't too thrilled with Jim "the cranky manager!" Consequently, the company sales, morale, and service took a nose dive. Managing a staff also exhausted Jim so much that the final dagger was little time for friends, family, or fitness. Was the promotion worth it? Nope! After a year of frustration, Jim returned to sales where he and his company were infinitely happier, healthier, and making more money.

Essential Takeaways
- Align your life and career with passion, purpose, and profits.
- Focus on what you do best — delegate, collaborate, or eliminate the rest.

The Importance of Team Alignment

Imagine a scenario where a football coach calls one set of plays, but his players execute strategies from a different playbook. Imagine further that the coach and players don't know each other's strengths and weaknesses because they've never practiced together. In fact, they don't even know each other's names. Sound farfetched? This occurs every day with project teams that work for the same company, but in different locations. This is a shame since individual and team goals must be in alignment for peak performance.

To assist you, I developed a self & team discovery system that identifies 12 *highly-connected Essentials* for life and business. This is the same system I use whether I'm coaching students, team leaders, or CEOs. If you also conduct this exercise with your inner circle, I promise you'll design a more crystal-clear alignment for personal and professional growth.

12-Point Self & Team-Discovery Tool

Step 1) Define Success & Purpose (clarify what makes you happy & why)

Step 2) Identify Your Individual, Team or Company Passions

Step 3) Identify Your Personality Styles (social, visual, creative, linear)

Step 4) Identify Individual, Team or Company Strengths (assets)

Step 5) Identify Individual, Team or Company Weaknesses (liabilities)

Step 6) Identify Your Individual, Team or Company Opportunities (primary focus)

Step 7) Identify Individual, Team or Company Threats (distractions, competitors)

Step 8) Identify Unique Individual, Team or Company Ability (your niche)

Step 9) Categorize & Prioritize Individual, Team or Company Goals

Step 10) Create Individual or Team Mission (what you do, for whom, and why)

Step 11) Create Individual, Team or Company Vision (future aspiration of mission)

Step 12) Identify Your Individual, Team, or Company Values for All Goals

CLIFF'S PERSONAL MISSION
"Love, learn, laugh, live, and give with passion, humility, and gratitude."

CLIFF'S TEAM MISSION
"Inspire, give back, and raise the bar for education and entrepreneurship."

Strategy 2
Master Emotional &
Communication Intelligence

> *"The most important thing in communication*
> *is to hear what isn't being said."*
> PETER DRUCKER
> Professor, Author (*Innovation & Entrepreneurship*)

What Drives Our People Skills?

IT WAS SOCRATES WHO said, "Know thyself," but it's equally important to understand friends, family, clients, teammates, and even strangers. Our ability to read people and situations is critical to effective careers, relationships, and leadership. To that end, let's build our social, emotional, and communication strategies around a few skills we touched on briefly in *Essential 1: Mindset 3 • Cultivate Creative Thinking* ...

1 Emotional Intelligence
Our self-awareness, self-discipline, and ability to manage emotions. This is a basic understanding of **what drives me**.

2 Social Intelligence
Our ability to empathize, get along, and read situations. This is a basic understanding of **what drives other people**.

Have you ever wondered how someone can miss facial expressions or verbal cues that would tell them how you're feeling? Could your own words and deeds be more clear, consistent, and constructive? Since communication is a two-way street, it never hurts to smile first, listen better, or make an effort to show you care. Anyone could be having a bad day. Things at home or work might be rough. Imagine what people don't know about you.

Everyone begins with basic needs of food, health, and safety. Career drivers include money and personal achievement. On our life journey, we hope for love, family, and a sense of belonging. The upshot to all of our social and emotional drivers is that we don't always have the same motives at the same time. This puts many people in potential conflict each day. So if quality communication and trusted relationships are the goal, we must be willing to learn about someone's past and present. YES, it's a BIG CHALLENGE to bring insight and compassion to all the people in our lives, but it's also worth it.

The Social & Emotional Solution
Building trust requires a conscious effort to care about others over an extended period of time, while staying in tune with yourself.

Social skills are influenced in part by family genes, how we were raised, and the people in our lives. What we eat and drink (sugar, salt, alcohol, caffeine, drugs) also has a serious impact. The same is true of sleep, stress, and exercise. It's all connected to brain function, mood swings, and energy levels. We also form opinions based on books, movies, and media. Sometimes we get it right, but we often judge too quickly without enough information.

For example, we might assume a business leader with strong verbal skills is a born speaker or natural salesperson. We might assume the same of a talented writer. However, the strongest voice can often misread situations, fail to listen, or turn people off. A shy person on the other hand can be just as socially intelligent, if not more, than their loquacious peers. Introverts often listen better and set their ego aside. Patience and humility enable greater awareness. The good news is that *anyone* can improve their social and emotional intelligence by listening, caring, and showing empathy. In turn, we create healthier lives, trusted relationships, and winning teams.

Word Choice & Body Language

In today's digital world, we communicate so impulsively with text and e-mail that it's easy to say things without considering the impact. These impulsive habits follow us offline too. For example, have you ever seen someone roll their eyes disapprovingly at a friendly barista who innocently forgot the whip cream on a grande-double-mocha-cappuccino-soy-latte? Although the barista could have made a mistake, the customer may have been in such a rush that they forgot to say, "Please add whip cream."

How about social media? With keyboards clicking at the speed of light, **what** we say is as relevant as **how, where, when, why,** and to **whom** we say it. These days, we're on record with every text or posted image, but messages aren't always clear and consistent. Does everyone give careful thought to their verbal arsenal on Facebook and Twitter? Of course not, but every message has colossal power to make a difference (for better or worse):

- Inspire or discourage people
- Mitigate or escalate conflicts
- Build or destroy relationships

If your life or business is an open book, it's okay to be a wild provocateur. Just don't be disappointed if the world doesn't get your humor or brand of politics. I'm not suggesting we have to filter every word, but as Abraham Lincoln said, "It's sometimes better to remain silent and be thought a fool, than to open one's mouth and remove all doubt."

Avoid Passive Aggressive Behavior

In psychology, passive-aggressive behavior is commonly known as an unhealthy personality trait where habitual patterns manifest negativity, stubbornness, resentment, and procrastination. Intentional obstruction of someone's expectations of you is an even more destructive action. Those who look for ways to sabotage important tasks or conversations inevitably do the most damage.

There are many justifiable reasons to remain silent or avoid tasks, such as fear, abuse, job loss, or legal threats. In most cases however, avoiding a conversation, going off topic, or using e-mail to evade serious conversations, only makes things worse. When in doubt, consider a neutral facilitator (friend or consultant) to moderate disputes and always remember this mantra:

> The best solution is in the dialogue.
> There's less power in a monologue.

The 10 Communication Commandments

Commandment 1) Master the Art of Listening
Don't interrupt. You learn more from what you hear than what you say.

Commandment 2) Communicate with Integrity
Say what you mean and do what you say.

Commandment 3) Consider the Social Media Effect
Be aware of your voice and know your audience.

Commandment 4) Deliver on 1st and 2nd Impressions
When meeting someone, ask what you can do for them and follow up. People will remember your second impression more than the first.

Commandment 5) Do Your Homework & Never Assume
Be prepared! You don't want to make an "ASS" out of "U" and "ME."

Commandment 6) Be Clear, Consistent & Constructive
S.M.A.R.T. > Specific • Measurable • Attainable • Relevant • Time-oriented

Commandment 7) Manage Expectations
Under promise and over deliver. He who promises most, performs least.

Commandment 8) Consider Your Delivery Options
Private vs. public • Online vs. offline • Formal vs. informal

Commandment 9) Always Be Polite & Grateful
Remember two phrases: "Please." and "Thank you."

Commandment 10) Monitor Your Messages
Evaluate your most recent e-mails, letters, posts, and conversations. Check content for word choice, branding, and communication intelligence.

Express Yourself The Best You Can

When I was in middle school, I knew my verbal skills could compensate a bit for my reading and writing challenges, but I spoke so fast that the words didn't always come out as intended. Fortunately, a miracle worker taught me the secret to seeing, hearing, and speaking as clearly as possible.

Born in 1880, a childhood illness left Helen Keller deaf and blind. She was closed off from the outside world the first seven years of her life with no means to communicate, other than unruly behavior and sounds of frustration. Keller's journey from a world of darkness to global recognition is as much a lesson in communication as one of courage.

By age 6, all hope was nearly lost, but Helen's mother read *American Notes*, a travel log by Charles Dickens that described the achievement of another deaf and blind child. Inspired by the Dickens story, the Kellers met a specialist who advised them to visit an expert in teaching deaf children. That expert was Alexander Graham Bell, inventor of the telephone. Bell suggested the Kellers contact the director of the Perkins School for the Blind. He recommended a former pupil named Anne Sullivan who the Keller family hired.

Sullivan first taught Helen to communicate by spelling words into her hand at the age of seven. Keller's voracious appetite to know the names and symbols for everything came shortly after. The rest of Keller's story was chronicled in a play and movie titled *The Miracle Worker*.

At age 24, Keller was the first deaf-blind student to earn a Bachelor of Arts from Radcliffe College. She went on to inspire millions of people as a prolific writer, lecturer, and social activist. Although she was never able to master speech due to inadequate teaching methods in her time, Keller exceeded a range of communication for a person so seemingly challenged. She published books, toured the world, and became a teacher. She met every President of the United States from Coolidge to Kennedy and won the Presidential Medal of Freedom for her social and humanitarian efforts.

I saw the movie *Miracle Worker* when I was 12 years old and it had a profound impact on my life. At the time, I was still very frustrated that reading was so hard for me, especially since I loved books and had a burning desire to be a writer. The Keller story inspired me to improve both my reading and writing skills. After all, if I could see, hear, and speak, what excuse did I have for not expressing myself the best I could.

Quality Before Quantity Relationships

Whenever I speak at a conference or university, I ask the audience for one-word definitions of a relationship. Positive responses are words like "friend," "trusted," or "romantic." Negative responses are words like "destructive" or "codependent." Business relationships often get described as "short-term" vs. "long-term" or "strategic" vs. "competitive." The more important questions I ask are, "Which relationships can you count on at 3:00 a.m.?" "Who will give you honest feedback when you do something wrong?" Those relationships are key.

Personally, I love hearing background stories about people. It provides so much insight to who they are, what they do, and why they do it. Taking a genuine interest in others is a strategy that requires learning and asking how we can be of service, while expecting nothing in return. If we get that part right, others will learn the most important thing they need to know about us — that we actually care.

When strong networkers are at their best, they simply listen, learn, solve, and share. This principle rewards us in terms of goodwill, new friends, and opportunities. What simple conclusion can we draw? The best networkers aren't big talkers — they are invariably the best listeners.

How to Network With Purpose

If quality networking is your goal, observe people the next time you go to a party or business gathering. Notice how some folks only shmooze with those they know (the comfort zone), while others collect business cards but never connect on a personal level. If you watch carefully, you'll also discover the most productive networker in the room. You'll know them the second you meet them because they smile, listen well, and make people feel welcome. They treat everyone with respect and connect strangers to one another, expecting nothing in return. When you see these lovable linchpins, don't be intimidated. They want you to say, "Hello." They actually live for "Hello!"

Effective networkers see everyone as a potential friend, client, or mentor. They're always caring and connecting. Don't be discouraged by people who don't have time for you. Simply smile and move on. Quality relationships take time, be it romance or high finance. Just make an effort to meet as many people as possible. Even competitors can be future partnerships, so take notes and follow up. If you tend to get nervous or don't know what to say when meeting new people, bring a friend to help break the ice. With practice, networking gets easier!

Honor Codes for Networking

With access to so many social and business networks online and offline, it should be easier than ever to meet people. However, the concept of *networking with purpose* often gets lost in our fast-paced world. For example, many Internet platforms encourage users to judge each other based solely on headlines and photos, but profile descriptions are subjective. We must be conscientious in the way we use and interpret social media, e-mails, calls, and face-to-face meetings. Your brand, career, and relationships depend on several honor codes.

5 RULES FOR "FACE-TO-FACE" NETWORKING

1) Ask friends and peers for warm introductions.
2) Introduce others, including strangers you just met.
3) Ask questions. Listen intently. Find common ground.
4) Offer to help others before asking for what you want.
5) Be patient. Trust takes time. When you care, they care.

5 RULES FOR "ONLINE" NETWORKING

1) Thou shalt not SPAM!
2) Ask permission if you're not sure where a boundary lies.
3) Keep text, e-mails, and calls short. Respect people's time.
4) Let new contacts know who referred you & why you're interested.
5) Be completely honest about yourself and don't gossip about others.

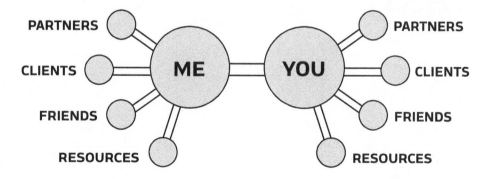

Strategy 3
Embrace Chaos, Decisions & Change

> *"It's not the strongest of the species that survives,*
> *nor the most intelligent, but the one most responsive to change."*
> CHARLES DARWIN
> Naturalist, Theorist

How Would Einstein Solve That?

IN EIGHTH GRADE, I did a book report on Albert Einstein and never forgot one of his famous quotes. He said, "If I had an hour to solve a problem and my life depended on it, I would use the first 55 minutes formulating the right question. Once I've identified the right question, I can solve the problem in less than five minutes." In other words, Einstein attached logic to the most visceral emotion he could think of — death! That was my first lesson on decision-making like a scientist (or an entrepreneur for that matter).

The secret to decision-making is asking intelligent questions. Sometimes we need deliberate thought for days or weeks. Other decisions require swift action, such as what to do when the house is on fire! The key is to avoid fear-based questions like "What if I fail?" A fear of failure doesn't provide clarity when time is of the essence, so let's explore a few solutions:

My 6 Favorite Starter Questions for Hard Choices

1) What does my gut tell me ?
2) Do I have the data to support my conclusion?
3) Is the required action in line with my mission and values?
4) Will this decision make me happy, healthy, wealthy, or wise?
5) What worked? What didn't work? What lessons were learned?
6) Can I get help, delegate the decision, and live with the outcome?

How Would Socrates Debate That?

If we journey back a few thousand years, we find the origins of problem solving with Greek philosophers such as Aristotle and Socrates. Aristotle credited Socrates with the scientific method (a body of questions or experiments used to prove or disprove a prior belief). Similarly, the Socratic Method for debating issues is a series of questions and answers between individuals used to stimulate critical thinking. The goal for each person in a Socratic debate is to show an opposing view that illustrates where an argument is flawed, ideally getting the opponent to expose their own contradiction. If you like playing Devil's advocate, then the Socratic Method is for you. It takes more time, but if intelligent conversation matters, this strategy helps your decision-making process.

How Would Benjamin Franklin Size it Up?

We only have to journey back a few hundred years to learn a simpler version of the Socratic Method, which is credited to American diplomat Benjamin Franklin. When faced with a hard decision, Franklin would draw a line down a piece of paper, listing rewards of a decision on one side, and risks on the other side. For example, let's say you're the CEO of an Internet start-up faced with two options for expansion: 1) organic growth; 2) merging with a larger company. The merger will bring plenty of new ideas, clients, talent, passion, and experience to the table, but it may also bring unforeseen baggage and cultural differences.

Which direction is in your best interest ...?

Merger Rewards	Merger Risks
• New assets & more revenue	• Unforeseen liabilities
• New clients & vendors	• Unforeseen bias & baggage
• New ideas & talented partners	• Unforeseen strategic differences
• New passion & enthusiasm	• Unforeseen value differences
• New experience & advisors	• Unforeseen creative differences

A merger is obviously more complex than a decision between vanilla and choco-late, so you may have to throw pros and cons on a whiteboard and have a Socratic chat with your team. A common mistake we've all made is trying to solve prob-lems beyond our expertise or experience, especially when we're emotionally or financially attached. In those situations, ask for help.

Essential Questions for Every Decision
1) What's the Mission?   2) Why are we doing it?

Cost Benefit Analysis

In the same way Einstein, Socrates, and Franklin would approach a prob-lem, always consider a **Cost-Benefit Analysis.** This is the basic prin-ciple of judging an opportunity cost (the value of making one choice at the expense of another). Whether you're a student on a budget or global entrepreneur, these three mission filters will always serve you well:

Time   >   Is it worth the hours or years?

Money >   Is it worth the dollars and cents?

Effort   >   Is it worth the energy and aggravation?

Key Reminders

Too many chefs in the kitchen can spoil the soup,
and sometimes you need extra brains in the board room.

Whatever You Do, Make a Decision

Even if you're on the right track,
you'll get run over if you just sit there.

Analyzing Crisis to Thrive on Change

Life is hard and bad things happen to good people, but the challenges most of us face will pale in comparison to billions of people who suffer without food, shelter, clean water, or education. Add physical challenges or a natural disaster to the mix and all bets are off. Nonetheless, every crisis presents an opportunity to build new skills, strategies, and perspective. Simply start with self-awareness:

- What am I feeling?
- What's my purpose?
- What are my resources?
- What changes are essential to survive?

To address these questions, behavioral experts often look at five stages of grief, identified by Swiss psychiatrist, Elisabeth Kubler-Ross (1926-2004). The Kubler-Ross theory was first introduced in her book, *On Death and Dying* (1969). The five stages are: **denial, anger, bargaining, depression,** and **acceptance**. As a method for dealing with trauma or loss, the grief model provides insight to how we deal with crisis, according to mindset and experience.

Although some psychologists debunk the Kubler-Ross Theory because the sequence between stages of grief isn't the same for everyone, recognizing the volatility of stages is essential to all of us, especially leaders, parents, and mental health practitioners. Some people skip denial and go straight to bargaining. Others go in and out of anger, depression, and acceptance, even years after a tragedy. Physical, neurological, or financial challenges may also affect an individual's coping abilities, especially if multiple challenges exist at the same time.

For example, I was speaking at a conference when the stock market tumbled in late 2008. Someone asked if I thought people were in denial about the cause and effect of the crash. The best analogy I could think of was the Kubler-Ross Grief Model. Spearheaded by the near collapse of America's banking, auto, and real estate industries, billions of people simultaneously spiraled into all five stages of grief, highlighted by denial, anger, and depression. Companies and countries woke up to tragic flaws in reckless financial systems and government practices. Citizens had fallen prey to investor schemes, mortgage fraud, and pitfalls of their own greed. Unemployment would rise to levels not seen since the Great Depression. Retirement savings were wiped out, years of hard work destroyed, and illusions of home values stripped away. Whether you were wealthy or poor, everyone responded with one of the five Kubler-Ross grief stages.

Stage 1 – Denial

EVERYTHING IS FINE. THIS ISN'T HAPPENING TO ME.

Long before the 2008 economic crisis, many people assumed that personal greed, non-sustainable debt, and fraudulent accounting could go on forever. Let's call this a collective DENIAL that kept an illusion alive for decades. It only took a few months after the crisis for the former Chairman of the United States Federal Reserve, Alan Greenspan, to acknowledge a flaw in his own financial theories. He said, "It was wrong to believe bankers, business leaders, and governments would be honest enough to regulate themselves." Greenspan and financial-policy makers also admitted that it was egregious to merely print money, deregulate banks, and manipulate interest rates in an effort to grow global economies. Even the "trickle-down economic theory" was debunked by the world's leading economists. (*Trickle-down economic theories suggest that tax breaks for big corporations and wealthy people will result in profits being re-invested in more jobs that benefit the poor and middle class, but there has never been substantive data to support the hypothesis*). As a result of these revelations from the "so-called experts," global citizens quickly joined Wall Street in a state of collective shock and DENIAL. For those who lost a job, a home, or retirement money, reality triggered STAGE 2: ANGER!

Stage 2 – Anger

WHY ME? WHO'S TO BLAME? THIS ISN'T FAIR!

Although corruption ran amuck in many countries leading up to the crisis, the expression "America sneezes and the world catches a cold," was never more apropos than 2008's financial heart attack. The collapse of Lehman Brothers (the 4th largest finance company in America) and the required bailout of AIG (the largest American insurance carrier (88 million customers in 130 countries) soon turned DENIAL into ANGER. Everyone pointed fingers at crooked corporations and inept governments, but very few people were willing to take responsibility for their own greed. In years to follow, serious changes in spending, borrowing, and regulations were imperative to avoid global bankruptcy by individuals, bankers, and governments alike. Since most people don't like change, it was time for STAGE 3: BARGAINING!

Stage 3 – Bargaining

I PROMISE TO BE GOOD. PLEASE LET ME LIVE TO PLAY ANOTHER DAY.

While no one had a perfect solution to the once-in-a-generation financial storm of 2008, the BARGAINING game of the century began. Everyone looked for handouts and started negotiating for their own survival. At the height of the panic, I found myself at the Ideas Festival in Aspen Colorado where the world's elite economists, entrepreneurs, educators, politicians, and policy makers gather each year to discuss global issues. In front of every serious thinker at the conference, Lawrence Summers (former Harvard President and Director of National Economic Council for President Barack Obama) said, "There are only two types of economists in today's world: 1) those who don't know; and 2) those who know they don't know." That was both hilarious and shocking. Welcome to **STAGE 4: DEPRESSION**.

Stage 4 – Depression

I'M SAD. I SEE NO SOLUTIONS. NO ONE UNDERSTANDS MY PROBLEM.
When people started losing jobs, homes, retirement money, or their business, the physical and emotional toll was so debilitating that millions of citizens fell straight into a prolonged **STAGE 4: DEPRESSION**. For many, that stage of grief can (and did) last for years. The goal in any crisis however is to move past the first four stages and arrive at Kubler-Ross Stage 5: **ACCEPTANCE**.

Stage 5 – Acceptance

I UNDERSTAND. I'M READY TO RECOVER.
ACCEPTANCE is the moment where an individual is ready to gain control of their life, and help others in the most clear-headed and constructive way.

4 Steps to Arrive at Acceptance

1) Be **humble** and ask for help.
2) Recognize the **benefits** of change.
3) Be **open-minded** so you can pivot as needed.
4) Gain **perspective**. Others conquered similar situations.

Handling a crisis demands strength, humility, and a leadership mindset. We have to show empathy as others go through denial, anger, bargaining, or depression (at their pace, in their way). As Martin Luther King, Jr. said, "The ultimate measure of a man is not where he stands in moments of comfort, but where he stands at times of challenge."

Strategy 4
Work With Teams, Leaders & Mentors

> *"Leadership is the art of giving people
> a platform for spreading ideas that work."*
> SETH GODIN
> Bestselling Author

Winning Systems

AS A TEENAGER, MY soccer teams were usually smaller and younger at international competitions, so we frequently lost to stronger and more experienced teams. On occasions however, we shocked the favorites with better tactics, conditioning, and commitment. The losing clubs usually suffered from overconfidence, weak leadership, and a poor work ethic. Those childhood lessons taught me a lot about playing with teams, leaders, and mentors who had proven systems that could stand the test of time.

The Miracle on Ice

At the 1980 Winter Olympics in Lake Placid, New York, a pack of unknown American college kids defeated a world-class Soviet Union men's hockey team. The victory was voted the greatest sports moment of the 20th century by *Sports Illustrated*. Several movies were based on the same story (*Miracle on Ice*, 1981) and (*Miracle*, 2004). Hollywood couldn't write a better script.

Was Team USA the most talented or experienced? Hardly. The college runts were considered no match for the mighty Russians, a professional team that had won the gold medal in every Olympics since 1956. The 1980 USA team were a bunch of amateurs, assembled only months before the Olympics. Hockey buffs and journalists described the match-up as boys vs. men and David vs. Goliath! Not only had the Russians defeated the National Hockey League All-Stars in previous years, they manhandled Team USA by a score of 10-3 in an exhibition game just two weeks before the Olympics. In early rounds of the tournament, the Americans would also be facing heavily-favored Sweden and Czechoslovakia. Team USA wasn't even expected to make the semi-finals against the Russians, let alone defeat Finland for Gold in the Finals, two days later, but for those unfamiliar with the greatest sports upset of all time — THEY DID!

USA Coach Herb Brooks knew his American boys didn't measure up on skill or experience. Brooks had been a player on the 1964 and 1968 Olympic teams which failed to even win a medal, but he had coached the University of Minnesota to three championships after taking over a losing program. Given his unique experience as a losing player and winning coach, Brooks knew the Russians were overconfident and susceptible to an American team, if he could get his players to believe in a selfless system anchored with purpose and national pride. "There would be no stars on Team USA," declared Brooks. With an average player age of 20, the American squad required self-sacrifice and zero tolerance for malcontents. Millennials may not remember the players, but the team mantra driven by Coach Brooks is still famous today:

> **"The name on the front of the jersey is
> more important than the one on the back."**

I had just turned 13 during the 1980 Olympics and was a huge hockey fan, but had never heard of a single player on Team USA. Nevertheless, their team mission was frozen in time. With the Americans leading 4-3, and moments to go in the final period against the Russians, I can still hear play-by-play announcer Al Michaels screaming at the top of his lungs:

> **"Ten seconds ... Five seconds!
> Do You Believe in Miracles? YES!!!"**

Headlines • Men's Olympic Hockey, Lake Placid, NY

Feb 22, 1980 • USA 4 – Russia 3   (Miracle on Ice • Semi-Final)
Feb 24, 1980 • USA 4 – Finland 2   (Gold Medal • Final Game)

Leadership Lessons From a Wizard

Growing up in Los Angeles, I had my pick of teams to root for and I followed them all from USC and UCLA to Dodgers baseball, Lakers basketball, and Kings hockey. I saw dozens of coaches come and go, but the greatest was one of my favorite life mentors, basketball Hall-of-Famer John Wooden (1910 – 2010), also known at UCLA as The Wizard of Westwood. Under his leadership, teams became legends and boys became men. He had just passed away at age 99 when I wrote this chapter. There were countless business icons I considered as leadership examples for this chapter, but no one compared to The Wizard.

During his reign, the Bruins won 10 NCAA championships in just 12 years, including 7 in a row. There were 620 career wins, 19 conference championships, and a home-winning streak that spanned 98 games. There were also 4 undefeated seasons (30-0), and a 4-year span that included 88 consecutive wins. These accomplishments were staggering for any coach, but if you talk to Wooden's players, they invariably point to his leadership principles first.

One former Bruin was Los Angeles Laker Hall-of-Famer Kareem Abdul-Jabbar. He won 3 NCAA Championships under Wooden before he became the NBA's all-time leading scorer, a 6-Time League MVP, and 6-Time NBA World Champion. When asked about The Wizard, Jabbar said, "It was an honor and privilege to learn life lessons from a man who made him a better leader, teammate, and human being."

In his bestselling book *Pyramid for Success*, Wooden describes what he feels are building blocks for winning. Ironically, Jabbar told Wooden he thought the pyramid was "corny" when he first saw it as a freshman. As a graduate, Jabbar acknowledged Wooden's brilliance. The basic tenets included enthusiasm, teamwork, humility, self-discipline, and an emphasis on personal character.

In 2002, Wooden was given the Presidential Medal of Freedom, the same award bestowed on pioneers such as Martin Luther King, Jr., Stephen Hawking, and Jonas Salk. In 2009, *The Sporting News* also listed the "50 Greatest Coaches of All Time" and to no one's surprise, Wooden was #1.

Top 10 Motivational Drivers & 10 Mojo Killers

Contrary to popular belief, money is not the only carrot to attract, inspire, and retain talented people. Whether you're a coach, teacher, or CEO, it helps to appreciate all the core drivers common to successful teams and individuals. As a leader, think about what motivates you and your tribe, then consistently ask if you're providing those incentives at every turn.

10 Motivational Drivers	10 Mojo Killers
• New ideas encouraged	• Same old, same old
• Fun & educational	• Painful and boring
• Advancement opportunity	• Dead-end job
• You get respect & recognition	• You feel ignored or disrespected
• You celebrate wins	• No progress in sight
• Great team environment	• No sense of belonging
• Emotionally rewarding	• No sense of purpose
• The work makes a difference	• No sense of contribution
• Positive environment	• Negative environment
• Financially rewarding	• Minimal incentives

Build a Trusted Forum

You don't need to be a CEO to build a personal brain trust or business advisory board. You can be a student, parent, professional, or committee leader. The key is your desire for growth and strategic excellence.

In my early twenties, I didn't appreciate how valuable a regular peer-to-peer meeting could be, but when I joined the Young Entrepreneurs Organization (known today as EO), I learned that a confidential Forum with team-driven protocols is the #1 system in the world for high-impact results. Dynamic forums are usually 8 to 12 of your most trusted peers who meet monthly to share personal and professional experiences. The protocols I teach were conceived over 50 years ago by the Young Presidents Organization (YPO). Forums are as effective for students and professionals as start-ups and large companies. Gestalt Language Protocol is a particular Forum tenet used for non-threatening and non-judgmental communication. Four such protocols that will benefit your Forum are:

1) Be as honest and specific as possible
2) Speak from personal experience rather than opinion
3) Establish clear mission, vision, and values for the group
4) Use "I did this" instead of "you should" in your comments

Advisory boards can bring tremendous value to a time-sensitive or start-up project. However, coaches, experts, and high-profile people are often over-hyped and under-utilized, so never give away equity or voting rights to your idea or business without benchmarks and accountability. Keep in mind that a game plan is not the reason most ideas or businesses fail. *Failure is often a lack of common values, work ethic, mission, and purpose among team members.* A trusted Forum can help you avoid those pitfalls.

Many Tasks & Many Mentors

Martial Arts master Bruce Lee said, "It's not the daily increase, but daily decrease of non-essentials that matter most." This quote taught me a lot, because I was definitely a Chief Everything Officer in my twenties. Trying to be the sales champ and company captain at the same time was a big mistake. Old habits were hard to break, but once I learned to delegate and collaborate, my personal and business life improved dramatically.

On your journey, find mentors who understand what's essential or non-essential to your mission. You want advisors who already succeeded at the level you hope to achieve. Also make sure there's a personality fit. If you're visual, you may not relate to someone who's highly verbal. If you're logical, someone who doesn't communicate well will drive you nuts. If you're lazy, you may need a drill sergeant! Many mentors know little about business and countless business mentors struggle to enjoy a balanced life. So-called experts have baggage just like you and me. So be sure to choose a coach who shares your values, passion, and purpose for each specific mission. You'll have many tasks in life. You'll need many mentors.

Meet My Virtual Mentor TED

The first TED conference started in 1984 to promote *Ideas Worth Spreading* in Technology, Entertainment, and Design. The initial conference actually lost money, but in years to follow, the scope broadened to include thought leaders from scientists, musicians, and athletes, to students, educators, and philanthropists. This diversity of ideas was prime for a digital age.

In 2001, media entrepreneur Chris Anderson became the Curator of TED, and by 2007, the speeches were such a phenomenal source of learning that free, online access attracted millions of fans worldwide. Once I got hooked, I made a habit of catching at least one TED Talk per week via TED.com.

My all-time favorite TED Talks (in no particular order) were by these inspirational game-changers: Sir Ken Robinson (*Do Schools Kill Creativity*), Dr. Jill Bolte Taylor (*My Stroke of Insight*), and Simon Sinek (*Start With WHY*).

3 Modern Leaders Who Influenced My Essentials

When I launched *The 4 Essentials (of Entrepreneurial Thinking)* in 2012, three peers that I highly respect were kind enough to endorse this book. Since they're all unique pioneers, I wanted to give them a shout out and share a few highlights from their respective # 1 *New York Times* bestselling books.

In 2010, I had just finished reading *Delivering Happiness* by Zappos CEO Tony Hsieh. The book highlighted corporate culture principles that were in harmony with *The 4 Essentials,* so I asked Tony if we could meet. After taking a tour of his headquarters, I learned first hand why Zappos was rated one of the top companies in the world for customer service and employee satisfaction. Ten Core Values helped Tony sell Zappos to Amazon for $1.2 billion dollars. The values are: *1) Deliver Wow Service; 2) Embrace Change; 3) Have Fun; 4) Be Creative; 5) Pursue Growth; 6) Build Honest Relationships; 7) Build a Positive Team Spirit; 8) Do More with Less; 9) Be Passionate;* and *10) Be Humble.* In short, a distinct system of highly-connected *Essentials* enabled Tony and Zappos to *Deliver Happiness.*

In 2011, I met Dave Logan, a former Associate Dean at USC's Marshall Business School and Co-Author of *Tribal Leadership*, an insightful book about how to lead successful teams and communities through mutual respect and self-less collaboration for greater good. I can't thank Dave enough for being such a positive influence on my work, and a generation of socially-conscious leaders.

I'm also incredibly grateful to Blake Mycoskie, Founder and Chief Shoe Giver at TOMS Shoes. Blake raised the bar for conscious consumerism by giving away a pair of shoes to a child in need with each pair of shoes sold by TOMS (One-for-One). Over 60 million shoes had been donated through 2016. When I met Blake in 2011, our offices were both in Santa Monica, California, so it was great to see the spirit of TOMS culture first hand. Inspired by the One-for-One campaign at TOMS, Cliff Michaels Global Learning provides FREE books and e-courses on life, career, and business skills to students, schools, and young entrepreneurs in need worldwide (**see: CliffMichaels.com**).

Thanks Again ... Tony, Dave, and Blake!

(Also see page 141, Essential 4: Purpose 4 • Give Back and Make a Difference)

Strategy 5
Focus, Set Goals & Manage Time

> *"The greater danger for most of us isn't that our aim
> is too high and miss it, but that it's too low and we reach it."*
> MICHELANGELO
> Painter, Sculptor

The Illusion of Time & To-Do Lists

THERE ARE 31,536,000 SECONDS in a year. If those were dollars and you had to use them, how would you spend your newfound wealth? After all, time is our most valuable, non-renewable asset and most people spend nearly one-third of life in bed. The rest is spent on a to-do list for work, play, health, family, friends, learning, and contribution to society. We're deluding ourselves if we think stuff happens just by writing goals in a day-planner. Phones ring, e-mails ping, emergencies happen, and people fail to show up. Each distraction can cause focus failure. We might even put up roadblocks to avoid negative people and projects (consciously or subconsciously), so there will be setbacks of our own making. In those moments where your mission meets madness, it helps to have a *Focus Mindset* baked into your game plan. The next story will give you time-tested strategies to stay on track.

Believe & Seize The Day

When I was 19, everyone told me to read Napoleon Hill's classic, *Think and Grow Rich* (1938). I was reluctant because the title sounded like every positive-thinking book out there. Nonetheless, I picked it up since millions of fans loved it, and I promised a mentor I would give it a serious look. I didn't even get past the first chapter before I realized it was a strategic blueprint to get things done, far more than the mere "*Think and Grow Rich*" title implied.

In 1908, a 20-something Napoleon Hill was a young journalist who landed an interview with industrialist Andrew Carnegie, one of the wealthiest men in the world. Carnegie encouraged Hill to research hundreds of successful men and women in hopes of discovering common threads for success. Over the next twenty years, Hill ended up studying everyone from Edison to Rockefeller. Carnegie believed the most common thread of these highly successful people was their mindset. Then in 1928, Hill and Carnegie co-published their findings under the title, *Laws of Success*. Ten years later, Hill published *Think and Grow Rich*, one of the all-time bestselling books. In time, Hill's name became synonymous with his trademark expression, "What the mind of man can conceive and believe, it can achieve."

In setting up the book's basic premise, Hill tells the tale of Edwin Barnes, a poor, uneducated man who had the gumption to hop on a train, and show up unannounced at Thomas Edison's laboratory, asking for an apprenticeship. Barnes made it clear that he didn't just want to work for Edison, but with him as a partner someday. Edison appreciated his tenacity and started Barnes with an apprenticeship. In time, Barnes got his big break when he noticed The Edison Dictating Machine sitting on a shelf collecting dust. Barnes was so positive he could sell the machine that he persuaded Edison to let him market the product. Barnes ended up selling the machine so well that Edison granted him nationwide distribution rights, and Barnes ended up making millions of dollars!

Moral of The Story
A man with no money or education was able to think and grow rich thanks to a positive mental attitude and burning desire for success.

Napoleon Hill said, "First comes thought, then organization of that thought into ideas and plans, then transformation of those plans into reality. The beginning ... is in your imagination." My take is that *Think and Grow Rich* could also have been titled *Believe and Seize the Day*. While positive-thinking is widely accepted as the main secret to Hill's classic, I'm convinced that Edwin Barnes' #1 success principle was being a man of action.

After all, who's likely to be more successful ...
a result-driven person or positive-thinking couch potato?

Your Strategic Mindset

1) Conceive & believe it

2) Use your imagination

3) Avoid procrastination

4) Acquire specialized knowledge

5) Build teams & fun environments

6) Make decisions & boldly go

Napoleon Hill wisely recognized that highly successful people often worked hard on days they didn't feel like it. As Actor-Director Woody Allen famously said, "80% of success is showing up!"

Goals vs. Greed • Beware of Wolves!

"Greed, for lack of a better word, is good. Greed is right.
Greed works. Greed clarifies, cuts through, and captures the essence of the
evolutionary spirit. Greed, in all of its forms ... greed for life, for money,
for love, knowledge ... has marked the upward surge of mankind ..."
MICHAEL DOUGLAS AS GORDON GEKKO
Wall Street (an Oliver Stone Film)

Oliver Stone's 1987 movie *Wall Street* included one of Hollywood's most memorable scenes. As fictional corporate raider Gordon Gekko, actor Michael Douglas delivers a powerful pitch at a shareholders' meeting, romancing "greed" in an effort to convince a corrupt board of directors that his hostile takeover bid is in the best interest of shareholders *and* America. The irony isn't lost on the audience since Gekko was as much the poster child for greed in the '80s as he would be for the 21st century.

In the film, ambitious but naïve stockbroker Bud Fox (Charlie Sheen) walks into a corrupt world when he pursues a job working for his idol, money mogul Gordon Gekko. Gekko takes the kid under his wing, but only if Fox will provide insider trading information (an illegal activity). Enticed by wealth and a high-society lifestyle, Fox succumbs to Gekko's allure of power and profits. He fails to see Gekko is only using him to destroy Bluestar Airlines, a company where Fox's father works and the source of his insider information. By the time he realizes he's a pawn in Gekko's scheme, Fox pleads with Gekko not to break up his father's company and put thousands of employees out of work ...

FOX: "...How many yachts can you ski behind? How much is enough?"

GEKKO: "It's not a question of enough ... Somebody wins. Somebody loses. Money itself isn't lost or made. It's simply transferred ... from one perception to another ... like magic, the illusion has become real. The more real it becomes, the more desperate they want it ... capitalism at its finest."

To make amends for his sins, Fox double-crosses Gekko by giving inside information to Gekko's arch rival. However, Fox is detected by legal authorities for insider trading (which he ironically learned from Gekko). In exchange for a lighter punishment, Fox testifies against Gekko, and they both end up in prison.

For Trivia Buffs

There are two films uniquely connected to the classic *Wall Street* thriller. Producer Suzanne Todd's suspense drama *Boiler Room (2000)* featured a corrupt CEO who inspired ambitious young brokers to peddle bogus stocks to unsuspecting buyers. The film was based on the real-world brokerage Stratton Oakmont, whose founder (Jordan Belfort) was portrayed by Leonardo DiCaprio in Director Martin Scorcese's Oscar-Winner, *The Wolf of Wall Street*. As an intensely greedy stock trader, Belfort's rampant fraud caused his downfall, just as it did for Gekko. Juxtaposed against each other, I drew two conclusions about these intertwined Hollywood flicks:

1) We all have big goals, but an ambitious Fox should never sleep with a slimy Gekko — that's scary crossbreeding!

2) There will always be Gekkos and Belforts in the world, so beware of wolves in sheep's clothing. Karma's a bitch!

Small is The New Big

Well-meaning business mentors love the mantra "Think BIG," but the phrase *"GO BIG or GO HOME"* may be the worst advice you ever get. People often fail at the smallest tasks by biting off more than they can chew. If it's true that less is sometimes more, then BIG purchases and material distractions can be a BIG waste of time, money, and effort.

In the business world, many BIG ideas never get off the ground because they require BIG partners or BIG capital. Sometimes it's better to start with baby steps. Prove your idea, build relationships, and make a few sales. Then you can attract those BIG clients, investors, or social media followers. You may also want to think about your personal bandwidth or ability to handle chaos. Are you sure you want BIG budgets, BIG payrolls, and the BIG bureaucracies that go with them? Smart leaders prefer less waste and small teams that can make fast decisions in dynamic markets. Some of the most successful lifestyles and business models are home-based and outsourced. So if simple is more your style, don't feel pressured to think BIG all the time. BIG companies may drive you crazy. If smaller makes you happy, less stress can be far more rewarding!

Plan A Versus Plan Q

Let's assume you've set goals, built great teams, and even assigned tasks. Can you still fail? Of course! In fact, bigger plans have even greater risk. Keep in mind that most people aren't working on Plan A. They're working on Plan Q for their careers, team goals, creative ideas, and product launches. Fortunately, there are 26 letters in the alphabet. Whatever you do, just stay busy. As Benjamin Franklin said, "Well done is far better than well said!"

- Talk is cheap. **Just do it!**
- Don't blame others. **Just do it!**
- Life is what you make it. **Just do it!**
- No need to check with 20 friends. **Just do it!**
- The world doesn't owe you a favor. **Just do it!**

---

10 Smart Rules for Better Work Flow

Smart Rule 1) Turn Off the Tech for a Bit
Unplug the TV, shut off the computer, and put down the cell phone.
Focus first and the world will happily await your glorious return.

Smart Rule 2) Write Goals & Plans with Purpose
List your goals, abilities, resources, needs, mission, vision, values.
(see helpful tools on pages 68, 96, 97)

Smart Rule 3) Categorize & Prioritize
Calls, tasks, meetings, health, finance, relationships.
Eliminate non-essentials (daily, weekly, monthly, annually).

Smart Rule 4) Delegate, Collaborate, or Eliminate
Drop the ego, ask for help, and team up.

Smart Rule 5) Schedule Your Day, Week, Month & Year
Create sacred time for work, play, fitness, friends, family, and learning.

Smart Rule 6) Commit to Your Unique Ability
Master core strengths. Don't be a jack of all trades.

Smart Rule 7) Seize the Day
Don't let perfect ruin good.
Start with one task that has the greatest impact on everything else.

Smart Rule 8) Assign a Focus Friend
Create accountability in your personal and professional goals.

Smart Rule 9) Optimize Your Environment
Clean up the mess if you want success!
(workspace, desktop, filing system, e-mails, social media).

Smart Rule 10) Celebrate Progress & Make it Fun
Add music, art, adventure, competition, or social impact to every goal.

Goal & Time Management Summary

Focus & Commit!

Goal & Project Planner (page 1 of 2)

Project _____ Start Date _____ End Date _____

Step 1 > Define Primary Goal & Key Objectives

Step 2 > Define Project Benchmarks for Success

Step 3 > Identify Required Partners, Teammates, Volunteers

Step 4 > Identify Project Leader & Responsibilities

Step 5 > Identify Required Tools & Strategies

Step 6 > Identify Experienced Mentors, Experts & Advisors

Step 7 > Identify Impact to Others Associated with this Project

Step 8 > List Key Starter Steps for Goal Execution (Day, Week, Month)

Step 9 > Establish Conduct Rules for Project & Team Members

Goal & Project Planner (page 2 of 2)

Step 10 > Conduct S.W.O.T. Analysis

Strengths	How Can We Leverage Resources?

Weaknesses	How Can We Improve?

Opportunities	How Can We Open Doors?

Threats	How Can We Solve Challenges?

Step 11 > Create Budget

Budget Item	Income	Expenses

Step 12 > Create Assignments

Member Name	Task	Benchmark

Lead Member Signature: _____

Focus Partner Signature: _____

Congratulations!

You've just concluded *Essential 2 Strategies* toward a **Master's** in **Basic Abilities.**

Here's a Recap of Your Top 5 Strategies

1) Take the Self Discovery Path

2) Master Emotional & Communication Intelligence

3) Embrace Chaos, Decisions & Change

4) Work with Teams, Leaders & Mentors

5) Focus, Set Goals & Manage Time

Essential 3 • **Values**

"When values are clear, decisions are wise."
ANONYMOUS

Align Your Values

I T'S NOW TIME TO align *Essential 1 (Mindset)* and *Essential 2 (Strategies)* to *Essential 3 (Values)*. When no one is watching or times are rough, what will you and your team stand for? Keep in mind that values selected for this book are merely a guide. You can substitute words like "truth" for "integrity" or "respect" for "gratitude". Either way, *Mindset* and *Strategies* must align with *Essential 3 (Values)* and *Essential 4 (Purpose)* for optimal success.

Master These 5 Values

1) Live with Integrity
2) Display Sportsmanship
3) Exercise Humility
4) Manifest Love & Tolerance
5) Show Gratitude

Value 1
Live with Integrity

> "It's never wrong to do the right thing.
> This will gratify some people and astonish the rest."
> MARK TWAIN
> Author, Humorist

Trust is Hard-Earned & Easily Lost

A S AN EIGHTEEN-YEAR-OLD ROOKIE in the real estate biz, I wore ripped jeans, talked too fast, and looked like I still belonged in high school. I thought, "Why would anyone trust a kid like me with their real estate transaction?" Nonetheless, I showed up on time, worked hard, practiced my *Essentials*, and wrote thank-you notes every day. It took a year before I earned my first client but she told me that my persistence (and chocolate kisses) sealed the deal.

I had many great mentors from friends and clients to strangers on the street who helped me realize the power of words and deeds. In recent years, I've also noticed that top schools and social entrepreneurs have made values a cornerstone of corporate-culture. To that end, I thought it would be interesting to put two of the wealthiest men in the world under the microscope to see if their words and deeds matched their public mission: Bill Gates (Founder, Microsoft) and Warren Buffett (Chairman, Berkshire Hathaway).

It's important to note that I'm not impressed with billionaires, even though I've discussed a few in this book. Some are worth emulating and many are not. I'm not a tech guy so my interest in Bill Gates was never about computers. I actually use Apple products (Sorry Bill). I don't buy stocks, so my interest in Warren Buffett was never a love for Wall Street (Sorry Warren). What I really wanted to know was why these two men joined philanthropy forces after they had already made their respective fortunes.

The $31 Billion-Dollar Question

*"To give away money is an easy matter and in any man's power.
Deciding who to give to ... how large ... when ... and for what purpose ...
is neither in every man's power, nor an easy matter."*
ARISTOTLE • PHILOSOPHER

FOUNDED IN 2000, THE *Bill and Melinda Gates Foundation* donates billions of dollars to global causes. The foundation was started to solve everything from malaria and global poverty to shortcomings in education and science programs. Then in 2006, industrialist Warren Buffett contributed $31 billion dollars to the *Gates Foundation*. Since the donation was unprecedented, I was fascinated to know why Buffett decided to trust Gates with such a large percentage of his accumulated wealth. After all, you don't spend a lifetime building a $31 billion-dollar nest egg, then trust it to just anyone.

Although Buffett has said he doesn't believe in dynastic wealth, such as leaving billions of dollars to his kids, it still begs a few questions: Why give all that money to Gates and what was the #1 qualifier? To find the answer, I turned to interviews and speeches the two men gave in many public forums following their partnership. First and most obvious, Gates and Buffett didn't become trusted friends because of a mutual love for computers on Warren's part, or a need for financial advice on Bill's part. When asked about how the two men formed such a unique bond, Bill and Warren invariably discussed alignment of values and purpose. Chief among their shared principles were integrity and gratitude.

MISSION STATEMENT: BILL & MELINDA GATES FOUNDATION

Guided by the belief that every life has equal value, the Foundation works to help all people lead healthy, productive lives. In developing countries, it focuses on improving people's health, giving them the chance to lift themselves out of hunger and extreme poverty. In the U.S., it seeks to ensure that all people, especially those with the fewest resources, have access to opportunities they need to succeed in school and life.

The Buffett-Gates alignment worked for many reasons, not the least of which were global resources and a mutual mission to make a difference. However, the biggest decision for Buffett boiled down to one core value that enabled him to size up Gates and say, "This is the guy I'm trusting with my $31 billion dollars."

For the final Buffett litmus test, I turned to a popular speech he gives to college students. He proposes a hypothetical scenario where students could invest in 10% of a fellow classmate's career. Before making a decision however, the students are asked which of three qualities they would consider most relevant to a classmate's future success:

1) Intelligence & Grades   2) Effort & Work Ethic   3) Integrity & Character

Buffett proposes that only one answer is logical — *integrity and character*. These are the same qualities driving his analysis of management teams when he invests in a company, or trusts someone like Bill Gates with $31 billion dollars. Buffett also reminds students that he would never hire a person who lacks character, and that integrity must be the foundation of our personal value system for others to believe in us. He ends the lesson suggesting that if each student built their principles on this fundamental belief, success would be limitless.

After concluding my research on Buffett, I turned my attention to Gates. His focus in later years clearly went through a renaissance from early days at Microsoft (when he was less altruistic as a young entrepreneur, fixated on dominating the software industry). In my study of Gates, I found a passage from a commencement speech he gave at Harvard, 35 years after dropping out. Just a few lines affirmed for me that Gates had evolved from a business-centric tech wiz to a social entrepreneur with greater vision. It was then that I believed Buffett made the right choice, for the right reason, at the right time in history.

"Taking a serious look back, I do have one big regret. I left Harvard with no real awareness of the awful inequities in the world ... the appalling disparities of health and wealth and opportunity that condemn millions of people to lives of despair. I learned a lot here at Harvard about new ideas, economics, and politics. I got great exposure to the advances being made in the sciences ... but humanity's greatest advances are not in its discoveries; but in how those discoveries are applied to reduce inequity."
BILL GATES – HARVARD COMMENCEMENT SPEECH (2007)

After reviewing the speech, I concluded that Buffett's decision to trust *The Gates Foundation* with $31 billion dollars was inextricably tied to Bill and Melinda's character. Bill's commitment to global philanthropy was even more evident in 2008 when he stepped down from his day-to-day role at Microsoft so he could focus more on the Foundation's mission.

The Giving Pledge

In 2010, Bill, Melinda, and Warren pushed the philanthropy envelope a step further. They issued a challenge to the wealthiest billionaires to pledge 50% of their net worth to charities during their lifetimes or upon death. If successful, this mission would change the face of global giving. In its first year alone, the Giving Pledge secured signatures from 40 billionaire-philanthropists. Among them are Joan & Richard Branson (Virgin), Sara Blakely (Spanx), Priscilla Chan & Mark Zuckerberg (Facebook), Jeff Skoll (Participant Media), Elon Musk (Tesla), George Lucas (Lucas Films), Ted Turner (CNN), Michael Bloomberg, David Rockefeller, and many others.

These days, finding integrity in global leaders is challenging. We've all watched the wealthiest men and women talk a good game (politicians, celebrities, business giants), but their words and deeds don't always match. In the end, Bill, Melinda, and Warren chose to leave the world with more than money — they will leave behind lessons in character and humanity.

Also see Page 141, Essential 4: Purpose 4 • Give Back & Make a Difference

Value 2
Display Sportsmanship

> *"One man practicing sportsmanship*
> *is far better than fifty preaching it."*
> KNUTE ROCKNE
> College Football Coach

No One Likes a Ball Hog!

GROWING UP IN LOS Angeles, I was blessed to watch hockey legend Wayne Gretzky (L.A. Kings) and basketball wizard Magic Johnson (L.A. Lakers). The thing that impressed me most about these iconic, MVP Champions was how much they shined the light on teammates. Magic didn't just throw an assist to James Worthy as he sprinted down court for a lay-up — Magic made James look good! As for Gretzky, it speaks volumes about his character that he had twice as many assists (1,963) than goals (894), both all-time records. He also won the National Hockey League trophy for sportsmanship five times.

In a world where profanity-laced tantrums from athletes and coaches are common, over-zealous parents are just as guilty for pushing kids to win at all costs. Don't even get me started on steroids, drugs, and tobacco in professional and amateur sports. Consider the damage we're doing to a generation of athletes getting mixed signals, even from Olympic heroes, where doping has been replete for decades. Whether you're a track and field star or corporate leader, you can cheat your way to money and fame or compete with integrity. You can win with style or jam it down someone's throat. These days, the line is totally blurred between winners and losers because sportsmanship is a lost art.

Fortunately, now and then, someone shows us the way ...

The Trip Heard 'Round the World

On July 26, 2008, 5' 2" Sara Tucholsky smacked her first career home run in a Division 2 NCAA women's college softball game. It was the last game of the season. The winning team would move on to play for a post-season championship. Sara's 3-run shot gave the Western Oregon Wolves an early second-inning lead. A backup right-fielder marred in a slump, Sara had just 3 hits in 34 at-bats all year — a meek batting average to say the least. She only started the game as a defensive replacement. The fact that this was her last game as a graduate and she had just hit her first home run was the kind of drama reserved for Hollywood, but Sara's home run was just the opening scene to an amazing story ...

GAME FLASH BACK >> Two runners on ... Two out ... No score ... Bottom of the second inning ... Here's the pitch ... Tucholsky swings ... it's a long drive to deep, left-center field ... the outfielder looks up ... it's gone! The crowd goes absolutely wild! Did little Sara really just hit her first home run?

Rounding first base, Sara misses the bag. As she turns back, her cleats jam, her body goes one way and her leg goes the other. In excruciating pain, she hits the ground. The rules don't allow teammates to help, so the scene is utter chaos as two runners score and Sara crawls back to first base. The umpire has never seen a home run where the runner can't complete a trip around the bases, and the rule book isn't handy, so he tells the Wolves' coach if Sara can't get up, the hit will be a 2-run single instead of a 3-run home run (*NCAA rules allow an injured batter to be substituted, but in the heat of the moment the umpire is confused*).

The opposing team are the Wildcats of Central Washington University. One of their players is starting first baseman, Mallory Holtman, a superstar and team leader in home runs, considered one of the greatest players in her school's history. Like Sara, Mallory is a graduating senior and this is her last shot at postseason glory. Ironically, Mallory would be facing double-knee surgery at the end of the season, but she postponed it in order to finish a run for a championship title.

As the umpire scrambles for a solution, Mallory says, "Excuse me, can I help her around the bases?" The first-base umpire confers with the home-plate umpire that there's no rule against a player from one team assisting another player, so the umpires approve the unprecedented moment. Mallory then signals to teammate Liz Wallace, who looks upon a teary-eyed Sara, still lying on the ground in pain. "We're going to pick you up and carry you around the bases," says Mallory. Sara approves the gesture and says, "Thanks." As Mallory and Liz lift Sara and begin the trip around the bases, Mallory says, "You hit it over the fence — you deserve it." As Mallory and Liz slow down to allow Sara's foot to tap each base, Liz says, "This has to look hilarious to everybody watching," and Mallory says, "I wonder if they're laughing at us." The three girls arrive at home plate and pass the torch to Sara's teammates who welcome her like she's just hit the winning home run in Game 7 of the World Series. A crowd in tears roars as they stand witness to a once-in-a-lifetime sportsmanship moment.

By the time Sara looked up, Mallory and Liz were back on the field, gloves in hand, ready for the next play. They expected nothing for their act of kindness, knowing it could cost the Wildcats their shot at post-season glory. Although Mallory had 2 hits and the Wildcats managed 2 runs, it wasn't enough. Sara's 3-run home run would prove to be the difference in a 4-2 victory. It was the first and last home run of her career.

In the media frenzy to follow, Mallory never considered her gesture special. She said any of her teammates would have done the same. Still, how many people step up when it counts? Deservedly, ESPN honored Sara, Mallory, and Liz with the year's *Best Moment* in sports at the 2008 *ESPY Awards*.

Sara's softball career ended that fateful day when she tore up her knee. Mallory continued to play softball after college, but a great part of the story followed shortly after. The two girls struck up a friendship, became motivational speakers, and started their own foundation to recognize those who exemplify sportsmanship.

Cliff's Game Rules

Rule 1) Let your game do the talking, not your mouth.

Rule 2) If you lose, move on. There's no crying in baseball.

Rule 3) Focus on the mission, not the madness of the moment.

Rule 4) Pass the ball. Goals & assists look the same on a scoreboard.

Value 3
Exercise Humility

> "When things are going well, be mindful of adversity.
> When prosperous, be mindful of poverty.
> When respected, be mindful of humility."
>
> GAUTAMA BUDDHA
> Spiritual Thinker

The Ego Challenge

NOW AND THEN, EVERYONE bites off more than they can chew, so regardless of ambition, humility lets us recognize what we don't know, aren't good at, don't like to do, or don't have time for. It enables us to say, "Perhaps I'm beyond my financial, emotional, or intellectual capacity." If we can be that humble, we tend to ask smarter questions:

1) What do I really need for success?
2) Am I listening to key people in my life?
3) Is it time to delegate or eliminate projects on my plate?

Humility wasn't something I learned from my parents. It was something I learned at different times, from different people, when I was mature enough to listen. Essential lessons were often subtle, but powerful. The key has always been an open mind, so I've tried to live my life by three simple rules:

1) No one knows it all.
2) No one can do it all.
3) There's always more to learn.

Are You the Tortoise or The Hare?

Most of us know the timeless lesson of "slow and steady wins the race" from Aesop's fable *The Tortoise and The Hare*. When I think of that story, a more valuable lesson comes to mind. A rabbit's life expectancy is less than ten years. The Galapagos tortoise can live to be one hundred and fifty years old. I'm not saying you need to put your money on the tortoise, but maybe the hidden gem in Aesop's fable is "Be patient, you'll live longer!"

At the same time, real-world deadlines will task patience every day. This is as true for career-minded students as it is for professionals who want to work hard, play hard, and breathe later. That constant challenge may cause conflict in our relationships, career choices, and life decisions.

The danger sign will be most apparent when your inner voice gives you extreme options at the same time (smaller, bigger, faster, slower). The truth is that short and long-term goals require that you sometimes be the rabbit, and other times be the tortoise. If you're still confused about which part of your brain should run the show, the following matrix may help.

4 Solutions to Battle Your Ego

Challenge 1	» You want it now but your gut says something's wrong.
SOLUTION 1	Slow down. Self-reflect. Be the Tortoise.
Challenge 2	» You believe you're right but most people say you're not.
SOLUTION 2	It's wise to learn & be open to new ideas.
Challenge 3	» You've been told you talk and brag too much.
SOLUTION 3	Speak less. Listen more. Drop the ego.
Challenge 4	» You hog the ball, so your peers are not inspired by you.
SOLUTION 4	Be selfless. Give others credit. Celebrate as a team.

"Little by little, one travels far."
J.R.R. TOLKIEN (AUTHOR, *The Hobbit, Lord of The Rings*)

"The two most powerful warriors are patience and time."
LEO TOLSTOY (AUTHOR, *War & Peace*)

Value 4
Manifest Love & Tolerance

> *"In the practice of tolerance, one's enemy is the best teacher.*
> *Our prime purpose in this life is to help others.*
> *And if you can't help them, at least don't hurt them."*
> 14TH DALAI LAMA
> Buddhist Monk, Peacemaker, Spiritual Leader

Compassionate Change-Mavens

CONNECTED MORE THAN EVER by social networks, we remain divided on many levels. I'm right, your wrong. The far left, extreme right. Throughout history, millions of people have been killed in the name of land, money, power, religion, racism, sexism, and homophobia. Oppression spans almost every region and religion of the world, where elements of greed and ignorance still breed intolerance today. With so much human intelligence however, why do we still struggle with the most *Essential* lessons of all?

Prejudice exists because each person is influenced by different parents, politics, values, schools, and cultures. Sometimes we inspire love and tolerance. Other times, we promote hate and fear. But if we can put a man on the moon and spend trillions of dollars on technology, we can certainly find ways to manifest love, heal the sick, feed the hungry, shelter the homeless, and educate every child.

Tolerance and conflict resolution aren't skills we learn overnight. These are tenets that nations have struggled with for thousands of years. Fortunately, there were peaceful mentors along the way, many who forged my views as a social entrepreneur. Among my favorite change mavens were Mahatma Gandhi, Nelson Mandela, Jackie Robinson, Rosa Parks, Martin Luther King, Jr., Muhammad Ali, and Malala Yousafzai. Each of these peacemakers fought for human rights when racist laws were stacked against them. In this chapter, I share their highly-connected walk through history.

The Great Soul

"An eye for an eye only ends up making the whole world blind."
MOHANDAS "MAHATMA" GANDHI (1869-1948)

Mohandas Gandhi was born and raised as a Hindu. His form of peaceful protest had tremendous influence on civil rights in his homeland of India and around the world. At 19, Gandhi studied law in London, but ultimately started his practice in South Africa as a young attorney. While there, he was appalled by discrimination that he not only witnessed, but personally experienced. He was beaten up on a train when he refused to give up his seat to a white passenger. He was asked to take off his turban in a courtroom, so he simply walked out in protest. These personal indignities inspired Gandhi to influence change, and as a lawyer in South Africa, he gained many legal concessions for local Indians. By the time he returned to India in 1914, his activism had earned the nickname Mahatma, which means The Great Soul.

By 1920, Gandhi was the most visible figure in the movement for Indian independence against an oppressive British regime. Arrested in 1922 for organizing movements, he was sentenced to six years in prison, but released in 1924 thanks to peaceful protests and growing awareness. In 1930, he launched a new civil disobedience campaign against the colonial government's tax on salt, a fee that severely affected India's poorest citizens. Then in 1931, Gandhi agreed to represent the Indian Congress Party (INC) at a Round Table Leadership Conference in London. Unfortunately, his movement had grown so powerful, that he was arrested by the new government.

In 1934, Gandhi announced his retirement from politics but was drawn back into the fray during World War II. Once again, he would lead the INC, demanding that Britain withdraw from India in return for cooperation with the war effort. Instead, British forces imprisoned the entire INC leadership. While in jail, Gandhi began hunger strikes to protest the mistreatment of lower classes, which he called "Children of God." Many of his followers disagreed with Gandhi's methods because progress was slow, but the strikes and civil movements resulted in many reforms in the Hindu community and government.

By 1947, Gandhi undertook more hunger strikes to increase awareness of oppression nationwide. His followers became so vocal that Britain eventually granted India its independence, but split the country into two territories: India and Pakistan. Gandhi strongly opposed the break, but hoped Hindus and Muslims would achieve peace among themselves after independence was declared.

Unfortunately, riots broke out in Calcutta. Urging Hindus and Muslims to live in peace, Gandhi led another hunger strike until there was peace in that region. Then in January 1948, Gandhi carried out another fast to inspire peace in Delhi, but was shot by a Hindu fanatic. The next day, a million people followed the funeral procession to the banks of the holy Jumna River.

Billions of people know the Gandhi mantra, "Be the change you wish to see in the world." It has become the most Essential lesson to manifest love and tolerance.

The Long Walk to Freedom

"Education is the most powerful weapon you can use to change the world."
NELSON MANDELA (1918-2013)

After studying Gandhi, my next peace mentor was Nelson Mandela, a human rights activist who served as President of South Africa from 1994 to 1999. As one of history's most compassionate warriors, Mandela brought an end to the oppressive apartheid regime which ruled for 50 years. His story connects every *Essential* in this book.

Mandela was born into a royal family of a small African village. His father was a tribal chief who named him Rolihlahla, which ironically means "troublemaker." At age 7, he was given the name Nelson by a British teacher. Mandela attended the finest schools, studied law, and was groomed for leadership at an early age. In 1941 (age 23), he began attending meetings of the African National Congress (ANC) and became a strong advocate for human rights. By 1952 (age 34), he was such a vocal threat as a black leader against a white government, he was banned from public speaking.

In 1961, Mandela co-founded a new wing of the ANC that was willing to take up arms, but only after peaceful protests were barred by the government. He would later reject violence as a means for solving the racial divide in South Africa. As Mandela's activism grew, he had to go underground to keep his movement alive. By 1964 (age 45), his profile as a human-rights champion had reached heroic stature, and he was prepared to be the sacrificial lamb his country needed. When he reappeared publicly, Mandela and seven of his most loyal followers were unjustly sentenced to life in prison for crimes against the government.

In 1976, young, black protestors were shot in the streets of South Africa and pressure quickly grew on the government to stop the injustices. From prison,

Mandela continued his rally cry for peaceful resistance. Nearly a decade later (1985), Irish songwriters and humanitarians Bob Geldof and Midge Ure produced the LIVE AID Concert to bring attention to millions of people starving in Ethiopia. The ripple effect was a global outcry for South African authorities to free Mandela and dismantle apartheid. Geldof and Ure co-wrote *Do They Know It's Christmas* (1984), which inspired songwriters Quincy Jones, Michael Jackson, and Lionel Richie to produce *We Are The World* (USA for Africa, 1985). Dozens of music icons from Phil Collins to Whitney Houston performed at Wembley Stadium in London and John F. Kennedy Stadium in Philadelphia. It was the largest peaceful protest in human history at the time.

Live Aid inspired The Concert for Nelson Mandela in 1988, the world's next largest peaceful protest with an audience of 600 million people in 67 countries. That same year, Amnesty International's Human Rights Now Tour featured Sting, Peter Gabriel, and Bruce Springsteen on a six-week concert series throughout Europe, Africa, Asia, and the Americas. When the tour reached Zimbabwe, the show was dedicated to Mandela and murdered black activist Steven Biko. Gabriel wrote a song titled *Biko,* and Springsteen urged white South Africans not to join the South African Army in "a country that was at war with itself." Consumers were also encouraged not to buy products or services from companies doing business with a corrupt and oppressive apartheid government.

The peaceful protests had a huge impact. After 27 years of wrongful imprisonment, Mandela was freed in 1990 (age 70). Over a half million people appeared to hear him speak and just three months after his release, he was elected to lead the African National Congress. By the time he was released, there was worldwide condemnation of apartheid. True to his core values for peaceful change, Mandela did not condemn the white leadership. Like Gandhi before him, he ushered in a new era of peace, unity, and tolerance between all races.

One of the more memorable stories of his time in prison was why Mandela befriended his jailers. He said, "If you want to make peace with your enemy, you have to work with your enemy. Then he becomes your partner." Within a few years of his release, Mandela was awarded the Nobel Peace Prize in 1993 and was the leader of South Africa for years to come.

It was a long walk to freedom, but love was the ultimate path to peace.

Breaking The Color Line

"Life is not a spectator sport.
The right of every American to first-class citizenship
is the most important issue of our time."
JACKIE ROBINSON (1919-1972)

Born into poverty in Cairo, Georgia, Jackie Robinson not only changed the face of baseball, he pioneered the Civil Rights Movement a decade before Rosa Parks and Martin Luther King Jr. helped change segregation laws in the United States. Jackie was the first athlete at UCLA to letter in four varsity sports (track, football, baseball, basketball). He was an excellent student but financial hardship prohibited him from getting his degree. It was a minor setback, so he pursued a football career in Honolulu.

Drafted to fight in World War II, Jackie had to put his athletic career on hold. Commissioned as a second lieutenant, his military service was interrupted when he refused to go to the back of a segregated bus in 1944. Jackie faced a court martial for the bus incident but was ironically acquitted by an all-white jury. Honorably discharged from the military, he had to start his career over.

Considering his options, Jackie joined the Kansas City Monarchs baseball club of the Negro Leagues in 1945. He was spotted by Brooklyn Dodgers' executive Branch Rickey who offered an opportunity to sign with the Dodgers' international farm club, the Montreal Royals. Jackie was selected not only for his athletic prowess, but his character. Breaking the 50-year color barrier as Major League Baseball's first African American player, Jackie was contractually obligated to "turn the other cheek" when faced with ridicule or death threats. On road trips with the Dodgers, he also had to stay in separate hotels.

Jackie was named Rookie of the Year when he turned pro in 1947. He also won the National League MVP award in 1949 with a batting average of .342. Within 5 years of signing with the Dodgers, 150 more black players were signed by minor and major league baseball, including Hall-of-Fame catcher and 3-time League MVP Roy Campanella. Jackie and Campanella were instrumental to the Dodgers winning their first Championship in 1955 against their arch rivals, the New York Yankees. Then in 1962, Jackie was the first African American inducted to baseball's Hall of Fame. For his contribution to the game and civil rights, Major League Baseball also retired Jackie's uniform "#42" across all major league teams. He was the first pro athlete in any sport to be so honored.

The First Lady of Civil Rights

"Each person must live their life as a model to others."
ROSA PARKS (1913-2005)

The United States Congress called Rosa Parks "the first lady of civil rights" and "the mother of the freedom movement." She was born Rosa Louise McCauley in Tuskegee, Alabama (1913). Her mom was a teacher who valued education, but since young Rosa had to care for her aging mother and grandmother, she ended school in 11th grade. At 19, she married Raymond Parks, a barber who was a member of the National Association for the Advancement of Colored People (NAACP). He supported Rosa and helped her earn a high-school diploma.

In 1943 (age 30), Rosa joined the Montgomery, Alabama chapter of the NAACP, and became the chapter secretary. Among her activities, she was an advocate for black voting rights. Twelve years later, on December 1, 1955, in Montgomery, Parks was coming home on a bus from a long day's work, and was arrested when she refused to give up her seat to a white passenger in the colored section (Factoid: she encountered the same driver 12 years earlier but left the bus to avoid a conflict). Like many brave, black women before her, Parks was arrested and lost her job by challenging the constitutionality of segregation laws.

Immediately following the incident, activists coordinated a bus boycott that lasted 381 days. It created a financial disaster for local business owners and the public transit system. Parks immediately became an international symbol of resistance to racial segregation at the same time that Martin Luther King Jr. had become the NAACP's official spokesman and a civil protest leader. In many ways, Parks and King inspired each other when King was just a young minister gaining national prominence. Largely due to their peaceful protests, The Supreme Court ruled that segregated seating was unconstitutional in late 1956.

Parks opened doors for everyone of color and was revered by human-rights activists. From 1965 to 1988, she served as secretary to John Conyers, an African-American US Representative and was also an active voice for political prisoners. Among her accolades, Parks was awarded the Presidential Medal of Freedom and Congressional Gold Medal.

"People always say I didn't give up my seat because I was tired, but that isn't true. I was tired of giving in."
ROSA PARKS

The March from Selma to Montgomery

"We must learn to live together as brothers or perish together as fools."
MARTIN LUTHER KING, JR (1929-1968)

Everyone should study the amazing story of Dr. Martin Luther King Jr., a Baptist minister and eloquent leader of the African-American Civil Rights movement in the United States. Like compassionate warriors before him, his mission for human rights centered on a message of love, unity, and non-violence.

A gifted student who attended segregated public schools, King was admitted to Morehouse College at age 15, where he studied medicine and law. He graduated in 1948 and was heavily influenced by Morehouse President Dr. Benjamin Mays (a theologian and civil rights advocate). After Morehouse, King entered Crozer Theological Seminary to earn a Bachelor of Divinity degree. He then enrolled in Boston University to earn a doctorate in theology.

King's family had been living in Montgomery, Alabama only a short while when activist Rosa Parks was arrested for not giving up her seat to a white passenger on a bus. King's voice for change during this critical time made him a target for white supremacists too. In fact, they ended up firebombing his home, but King and his family fortunately survived.

After the Supreme Court ruled that segregated seating on public buses was unconstitutional, King and his followers began the Southern Christian Leadership Conference (SCLC) in 1957. Their mission was to achieve racial equality through nonviolence. In his role as SCLC president, King traveled the world, gave lectures, and engaged other political leaders. During a trip to India in 1959, he met followers of Gandhi, who King described in his autobiography as "the guiding light of our technique for non-violent social change." Like Gandhi, King used boycotts, sit-ins, and marches to protest everything from segregation to unfair hiring practices used against African Americans.

On August 28, 1963, King worked with a number of protest groups to organize the March on Washington for Jobs and Freedom, a peaceful rally attended by 250,000 protestors. This is where King delivered his famous "I Have a Dream" speech that promoted love, peace, and equality, for all men, women, and children. The speech was delivered on the steps of the Lincoln Memorial (symbolic of a president who fought to end slavery in the United States). In 1964, King became the youngest person to win the Nobel Peace Prize, and The March on Washington influenced passage of the 1964 Civil Rights Act.

By 1965, King's international profile created a clash between white segregationists and peaceful demonstrators in Selma, Alabama, where the SCLC and Student Nonviolent Coordinating Committee had organized a voter registration campaign. The riots against their peaceful protests outraged many Americans and inspired King supporters across the country to gather in Selma and march to Montgomery. That year, Congress finally passed the Voting Rights Act for African Americans. Then in 1968, just as King was planning another march to Washington, D.C. (called the Poor People's Campaign), he was assassinated by gun fire on the balcony of a motel in Memphis, Tennessee.

For his courage and legacy, King was posthumously awarded the Presidential Medal of Freedom. In 1983, Martin Luther King Jr. Day was also established as a federal holiday by President Ronald Reagan. Although we lost another great leader in his prime, King's work inspired a generation of artists, athletes, and activists. The global concerts that brought attention to Mandela's cause and the abolition of apartheid in South Africa are just a few examples of the activism inspired by Dr. King. He also inspired a poetic, young boxer named Cassius Clay to fight for human rights and carry the peace torch for generations to follow.

The Greatest of All Time

"I'd like for them to say, he took a few cups of love, 1 tablespoon of patience, 1 teaspoon of generosity, 1 pint of kindness, 1 quart of laughter, 1 pinch of concern, and mixed willingness with happiness. He added lots of faith and stirred it up well. Then he spread it over a lifetime and served it to every deserving person he met."
MUHAMMAD ALI (1942-2016)

Born Cassius Clay in Louisville, Kentucky, Muhammad Ali was such an original hero, we may never again see a poet, athlete, and activist so eloquently personified as "The Greatest." After winning a Gold Medal in the 1960 Olympics, and becoming Heavyweight Champion of the World, Ali was in the prime of his career. Then in 1967 (age 25), he placed himself at the center of the civil rights movement, protesting the Vietnam War. Refusing to be drafted, Ali faced up to five years in prison and made the following political statement:

"I'm not going 10,000 miles to help murder, burn, and drop bombs on brown people in Vietnam, while so-called Negro people in Louisville are treated like dogs and denied simple, human rights."

As a result of his political protest, the New York State Athletic Commission stripped Ali of his boxing license and Heavyweight Title. With conflict at home and abroad, he was immediately criticized for changing his name to Muhammad Ali, but made the decision to denounce Cassius Clay as his slave name and stand by his Muslim principles. Public support was mixed as he spoke out against the Vietnam War and segregation at home, but a groundswell of Americans began to support Ali.

While his case was up for appeal, the Supreme Court finally determined that the Athletic Commission had unjustly ruled against Ali, so the charges were reversed, and his boxing license was reinstated. Although he was robbed of prime boxing years, Ali regained the Heavyweight Title from boxer Joe Frazier in 1971.

Then in 1974, Ali beat an undefeated George Foreman in Zaire, Central Africa. Aptly named the Rumble in The Jungle, his victory over Foreman launched Ali's international stature as a civil rights activist to new heights. In time, Ali became one of the most beloved sports figures as a 3-Time World Champion, was honored by Sports Illustrated as The Greatest Athlete of the 20th century, and was awarded the Presidential Medal of Freedom. When he lit the torch to open the 1996 Olympic Games in Atlanta, he also left us with an indelible memory as a global peacemaker.

The Girl Who Stood Up for Education

"One child, one teacher, one book, and one pen can change the world."
MALALA YOUSAFZAI (1997-)

Born July 12, 1997 in the Swat District of north-west Pakistan, Malala Yousafzai was named after Malalai, a Pashtun heroine who was known in a tale for providing soldiers with courage. Her father, Ziauddin, was an education activist who ran a school near the family's home for countless students who would otherwise have no school.

Ziauddin was an outspoken opponent of the Taliban terrorist group, and their efforts to stop girls from going to school. In 2009, as the Taliban's military hold on the area intensified, Malala began writing a blog for the BBC Urdu, under a pseudonym. She shared her father's passion for learning and expressed fears that her school would be attacked. Television and music were banned, women were prevented from shopping, and her father was told to close his school. Malala and her father received death threats, but continued to speak out. Around this time, Malala was featured in a New York Times documentary which revealed she was the author of the BBC blog. For her courage, Malala received Pakistan's first National Youth Peace Prize in 2011 and was nominated by Archbishop Desmond Tutu for the International Children's Peace Prize. In response to her rising popularity and national recognition, Taliban leaders voted to kill her.

On October 9, 2012, as Malala and her friends were traveling home from school, a masked gunman entered their bus and asked for Malala by name. She was shot with a single bullet which went through her head, neck, and shoulder. Malala survived but was in critical condition for months. The Taliban's attempt to kill her received worldwide condemnation and led to protests across Pakistan. Weeks after the attack, over two million people signed a petition for education rights, and the National Assembly swiftly ratified Pakistan's first Right-to-Free-and-Compulsory Education Bill.

As her crusade continued, Malala went on to become a passionate advocate for over 60 million girls worldwide who are denied a formal education because of gender. In 2013, she and her father co-founded the Malala Fund to bring awareness to the social and economic impact of empowering all girls to raise their voices, demand change, and unlock their potential. In 2014, Malala accepted the Nobel Peace Prize and contributed her $1.1 million-dollar prize money to financing a secondary school for girls in Pakistan.

Solutions Are in Dialogues, Not Monologues

In 2007, a Holocaust survivor named Shana shared her story with me over dinner. Her family was executed by the Nazis when she was a child during World War II and she was taken to a concentration camp. Shana survived the horror, but surprisingly harbored no hatred as an adult. I asked, "Why aren't you angry?" Shana replied, "**We must never forget the past, but teach, love, and forgive in the present. Solutions are in the dialogue, not the monologue.**" She also reminded me that millions of people have no books, free speech, or access to the Internet. "Since there will always be people who lack knowledge and compassion, it is incumbent on us to manifest love, tolerance, and education."

The great peacemakers taught us that we have more to gain by uniting others for the right reasons than excluding them for the wrong reasons. When we judge too quickly, we miss opportunities to meet amazing people and prosper from their wisdom. Intolerance also isolates us from one another, breaking down communication and any chance for resolution. Given the many benefits of teaching tolerance, it's my core belief that every school and corporate-training program should include these *Essentials* as much as any other life skill.

My Top 10 Tips for Global Peace & Prosperity

Tip 1) Speak softer, not louder

Tip 2) Listen with the intention of learning

Tip 3) Share ideas but don't insist on your opinion

Tip 4) Make the first concession and expect nothing in return

Tip 5) Turn the other cheek when intolerance is directed at you

Tip 6) Don't assume you know everything from first impressions

Tip 7) Shower enemies with love, compassion, and chocolate kisses

Tip 8) Leave the door open for future dialogue when you disagree

Tip 9) Make a genuine effort to know someone by asking questions

Tip 10) Remember that solutions are in the dialogue, not the monologue

14th Dalai Lama

Mohandas Gandhi

Nelson Mandela

Jackie Robinson

Rosa Parks

Martin Luther King Jr.

Muhammad Ali

Malala Yousafzai

Value 5
Show Gratitude

> *"You cannot do a kindness too soon because*
> *you never know how soon it will be too late."*
> RALPH WALDO EMERSON
> Poet, Philosopher

The Happy Dancing Lady

In 2007, I was on sabbatical in South East Asia, where an old woman with a careworn face was giving free dance lessons near my hotel in Phuket, Thailand. The local villagers told me she didn't speak, so they just called her "The Happy Dancing Lady." Her smile and energy were so engaging that crowds gathered to dance and take pictures. On my way to the beach, I decided to learn a little salsa from this old soul who was sharing her passion with the world. When the dance was done, she took my hand and gestured for me to tip a little boy who was sweeping around his mother's fruit stand. As I handed them money, the mother and child bowed in my direction and said, "Namaste."

I had just arrived from Los Angeles and couldn't wait to see what else Asia had in store for me. A few days later, I wasn't disappointed ...

Hello Stranger, You're Invited!

The day after my visit to Thailand, I was in Penang, a beautiful island off the northwest coast of Malaysia. I checked into my hotel, went for a hike, and came across a humble house in the hills, where a boy and girl were chasing a chicken in their front yard. With a wide grin, the boy greeted me as if it was his job, "Welcome to Penang. I'm Adil and this is my sister, Lily." Impressed by the young boy's hospitality, I replied, "My name is Cliff and it's very nice to meet you both!"

I then pointed to the chicken and asked, "What's his name?" Lily said, "Don't mind him. He's just dinner." The three of us then busted out laughing!

The kids kicked a soccer ball to me and were humored when I trapped it on my nose like a circus seal (soccer tricks are goodwill around the world). Their father Ahmad showed up a few minutes later and greeted me by name, "Hey, Mr. Michaels!" He was the hotel manager where I was staying, and so grateful that I played with his kids, he invited me to his cousin's wedding that night.

Just before sunset, Ahmad's family and I walked along a dirt road and arrived at a beautiful home nestled in the mountains. Flaming candles lined a pathway to a large porch where dozens of people were laughing, playing guitar, and sharing stories. Ahmad introduced me as his "#1 Soccer Pal from America" as if he had known me his whole life.

After the wedding ceremony, there was an amazing feast and I was humbled by the warmth of genuine new friends. As dessert was served, the newlyweds (Sarah and Kamal) addressed everyone by name and shared how each guest had meaning in their lives. They expressed appreciation for their loyal friends, loving parents, and generous grandparents. Imagine my surprise when they asked me to stand up and told everyone it was an honor to make a distant traveler welcome in their home and country. They said I reminded them of a family member they had recently lost, and that my visit was a well-timed blessing. In perfect harmony with hands on hearts, everyone in the room bowed their heads in my direction. Behind a stream of tears, I returned the bow and thanked them for a memorable evening of love, laughter, and friendship.

The hospitality bar was raised.
My life was never the same.

Love
Laughter
Friendship

Why 87% of the World Should be Grateful

There are 7 billion people in the world and one billion of those are living in poverty. Another billion people have no access to clean water, education, health care, or basic human rights. In *Essential 4 (Purpose)*, we'll discuss more about how we can make a difference by giving back, but don't forget to express gratitude for the people in your life and strangers along the way.

Special Thanks to Sarah, Kamal, and Ahmad in Penang!
... and The Happy Dancing Lady in Phuket!

Appreciation Tip 1) Say It!
There's no substitute for: "Thank you!" "I love you!" "You look great!"

Appreciation Tip 2) Personalize It!
A handwritten note or simple gift never goes out of style.

Appreciation Tip 3) Display Affection!
Gifts will never do when a hug or kiss is essential!

Gratitude Poem (*2007, South-East Asia Retreat*)

I'm thankful for failures. They teach lessons.
I'm thankful for challenges. They build character.
I'm thankful for what I have. Too much would be a burden.
I'm thankful for what I don't have. It shows what's possible.
I'm thankful for where I am. It's where I'm supposed to be.

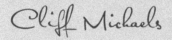

Congratulations!

You've just concluded *Essential 3 Values* toward a **M**aster's in **B**asic **A**bilities.

Here's a Recap of Your Top 5 Essential Values

1) Live with Integrity

2) Display Sportsmanship

3) Exercise Humility

4) Manifest Love & Tolerance

5) Show Gratitude

Essential 4 • **Purpose**

*"The meaning of life is to find your purpose.
The purpose of life is to give it away."*

PABLO PICASSO
Painter

Align Your Purpose

I N *Essential 1*, YOU mastered five *Mindsets*, starting with a definition of success and happiness. In *Essential 2*, you mastered five *Strategies*, beginning with a self-discovery path. In *Essential 3*, you mastered five *Values*, beginning with integrity. In *Essential 4*, our journey concludes with the simple premise that success and happiness come easier, and are infinitely more fun, when aligned with five *Purpose Principles* (the reason WHY you do it).

Master These 5 Purpose Principles

1) Ignite Your Personal Power
2) Follow Your Passion
3) Develop a Healthy Mind, Body & Soul
4) Give Back & Make a Difference
5) Enjoy the Journey

Purpose 1
Ignite Your Personal Power

> *"When I was five years old, my mother told me happiness was the key to life.*
> *At school, they asked me what I wanted to be when I grew up.*
> *I wrote down happy. They told me I didn't understand the assignment.*
> *I told them they didn't understand life."*
>
> JOHN LENNON
> British Singer-Songwriter -Humanitarian

E VERYONE HAS MOMENTS OF doubt when personal power is lost. Along the way, no one intends to sell their soul, but we all know a person who rented it for a while. Sometimes life is unfair and other times we need to acknowledge toxic elements we choose. The trick is to recognize our higher purpose and get back on track with *Essentials* that serve us best.

So how do we find that personal power when inner voices tell us we're tired or not good enough? The best solution is to break the negativity cycle. Paralyzing phrases like "I can't" or "It's too hard" must be replaced with healthier chatter, like "I will" and "I can." YES, practicing new verbal HABITS is intense work, but worth it. CHANGE can even be fun if you find your favorite path!

In my thirties, I took up yoga due to stress and sports injuries. I learned to sit still and listen to my true voice through meditation. If I'm having a bad week, I try to change my internal dialogue, even if it's just a five-minute positive mantra or visualization exercise. I might say, "This will be an amazing day filled with laughter and creativity."

The mind will act on what it sees, hears, and repeats, so I write daily goals, walk my dog to clear my head, and start each morning with an inspirational quote or song. Most importantly, I invite my inner circle to call "Bullshit" if they see me cheating on my authentic self. One of those friends was a yoga teacher who not only reminded me to breathe deep when I was out of focus, but shared his uncommon path to personal power ...

A Yogi's Journey to Bend Mind, Body & Soul

For years, friends and I would line up 30 minutes early to ensure a spot in Vinnie Marino's class at Yoga Works in Santa Monica, California. If you've ever been to a yoga festival, you know what I'm talking about. Even celebrities like Robert Downey Jr., David Duchovny, Heather Graham, and Kate Hudson would travel far and wide for Vinnie's music-infused Vinyasa, Ashtanga, and Iyengar yoga.

As a hundred students wait for class to begin, restless chatter would bounce off the walls. For hardcore yogis looking to bend their mind, body, and soul, the Vinnie experience is a unique challenge. If you're a newbie like I was, you'll regret leaving home without a water bottle — I barely survived the first 30 minutes, let alone the whole 90-minute class! I had to learn the difference between breathing ... and breathing deep.

The moment Vinnie walks in the studio, he cracks a joke or shares something going on in his life, making his personal ups and downs relatable to everyone. He then reminds us to focus on our intention and block out distractions. He starts us off with light stretches, but we're soon dripping sweat from intense poses and flow. Vinnie then cranks up inspirational music to a decibel you might expect at a night club, but it works. He plays everything from The Beatles and Rolling Stones to funk and acoustic. He also brings a different music play-list to each class so the lyrics and themes are never the same. It's an addicting workout, but Vinnie's high-impact classes are only half the reason for his loyal following and well-earned respect.

An Italian-American who grew up in New York, Vinnie is soft spoken but his methods for self-awareness are as meticulous as his yoga practice. At an early age, he developed a passion for yoga watching classes on TV. Drawn to meditation and spiritual authors, Vinnie convinced his parents to enroll him in a progressive high school that fostered alternative gym classes like yoga. It was the '70s, so Vinnie was also influenced by a drug culture and hippie generation in search of enlightenment. As a result, substance abuse started in his early teens. His yoga practice faded as drug exploration intensified. Drugs were a way to feel open and free, but for a spiritual soul like Vinnie, it was a dead-end lifestyle. Fortunately, Vinnie found sobriety by his mid-20s and continued searching for a greater purpose in life.

In his youth, Vinnie's yoga was traditional, but a move to Los Angeles in the early '90s reconnected him with a more intense practice that included music, spirituality, and a physical challenge. This reawakened his desire for personal power and growth. Vinnie was now high on his true drug of choice — YOGA! Serendipity played a hand next as Vinnie became an assistant to Hall-of-Fame rock 'n' roller Grace Slick, the lead singer of Jefferson Airplane. Slick was so impressed with Vinnie's east-coast spirit and passion for yoga, she encouraged him to build a career around his true calling. The next thing Vinnie did was blend his passion for great music with an intense yoga flow that even the most talented yogis find challenging. Coupled with his dry sense of humor and non-judgmental wisdom, Vinnie always has students laughing and thinking as they sweat. For me, that was his gift of personal power.

Myth Buster & 4 Personal-Power Habits

We've all heard that you're as successful as the 5 people you surround yourself with. That mantra is well-intended, but grossly inaccurate sometimes. Your 5 best business mentors might have no sense of life balance. Your 5 best friends may not be happy or successful in their careers, but can still be your most loyal companions. Your 5 favorite co-workers may share the bulk of your day, but that doesn't make your family less relevant. To accelerate personal and professional growth, practice The 4 Power Habits below ...

Habit 1) Maintain a Healthy Mind, Body, and Soul
Exercise. Eat well. Find balance. Create personal happiness before trying to make everyone else happy. Hang out with health buddies along the way.

Habit 2) Baby Steps Before Giant Leaps
Read or watch something new and inspirational each day,
then take action on one thing, rather than too much at once.

Habit 3) Keep Your Routine Positive
If you think you can or can't, you're right! Speak, think, and write positive words. Eliminate negative people who don't serve your purpose.

Habit 4) Include the Right People for The Right Journey
You can always benefit from different forms of wisdom, love, and humor. For life and career missions, try to diversify your most trusted mentors.

Purpose 2
Follow Your Passion

> *"My mission in life is not merely to survive, but to thrive ...*
> *and to do so with some passion, compassion, humor, and style."*
> MAYA ANGELOU
> Poet, Historian

Know Why You Do It

THE #1 SUCCESS PRINCIPLE described by happy and successful people is to follow your passion. Do the thing that drives you out of bed and you'll live a healthier, more fulfilling life — GUARANTEED! Everyone has to pay their dues so don't be discouraged if you're not in your ideal career or relationship yet. Just as your purpose may change, your passions may change at different stages in life. Yesterday may have been about art and innovation. Today might be about travel and adventure. Tomorrow could be about family or changing the world. Either way, follow your passion by engaging as many *Essentials* as possible *(mindset, strategies, values, purpose)*. Focus, care the most, and be the director of your story!

Lights, Camera, Action!

Growing up, I was a movie junkie influenced by many Directors. In my teens, Director John Hughes made coming-of-age stories (*The Breakfast Club, Ferris Bueller's Day Off*) which empowered teenage misfits. When I was 22, Director Peter Weir's *Dead Poets Society* introduced me to the Latin phrase "carpe diem" (seize the day) and that gave me a rally cry for daily goals. And my all-time favorite Director was Steven Spielberg. He not only introduced me to sharks, aliens, and dinosaurs, he taught me the importance of being the director of my story.

Funny thing about Spielberg's personal story is that he was a misfit too ...

Born in 1946, Spielberg started making 8-millimeter films with friends when he was just 12 years old. He was a C-average high school student, rejected three times by USC's cinema school. Thirty-five years later, Spielberg received an honorary degree from USC for his contributions to film and society. When I heard how Spielberg's journey came full circle, I thought it would be fun to share his essential back story for those who don't know the folklore.

As Spielberg recalls in interviews, he was taking the Universal Studios Tour during the college summer he spent at Long Beach State College. He had the nerve to jump off the studio tour bus, hide behind a sound stage, and stay on a movie lot all day. He went to make a phone call and bumped into the head of the Universal film library, Chuck Silvers. Spielberg wasted no time sharing his passion to be a filmmaker. Silvers was so impressed, he gave the aspiring young director a three-day studio pass so he wouldn't have to sneak around. Spielberg returned the next three days entering through the main gate, showing his pass to a security guard named Scotty. On the fourth day, dressed in a suit and tie, Spielberg was carrying his father's briefcase, filled with nothing but a sandwich. Rather than show his expired pass, Spielberg merely waved to Scotty who let him in. For the next three months, it was the same routine each day. The rest of that summer, Spielberg hung out on movie sets doing gopher work and learning the business. As Spielberg tells the tale, he once roamed on to the set of Alfred Hitchcock, hoping to learn from the master director of suspense. Unfortunately, young Steven was spotted and kicked out!

By 1968 (age 21), Spielberg had written a number of short scripts, including a 24-minute silent love story titled *Amblin*. By then, Silvers had introduced Spielberg to a friend named Dennis Hoffman who ran a special-effects lab. Hoffman was so impressed with Spielberg's short films that he invested $10,000 dollars to fund *Amblin*. Shortly after, executives at Universal had a chance to see Spielberg's body of work. Once they did, a 22-year-old Spielberg inked a 7-year television deal, making him the youngest director signed by a major studio. The rest is Hollywood history.

Spielberg films have grossed billions of dollars. His Academy-Award winners such as *Schindler's List* (1983) and *Saving Private Ryan* (1998) are only exceeded by his record-breaking box-office adventures such as *Jaws* (1975), *Raiders of the Lost Ark* (1981), *E.T.* (1982), *Hook* (1991), *Jurassic Park* (1993), and *Transformers* (2007). His global philanthropy and pioneering films also earned Spielberg a spot on *TIME Magazine's* 100 Most Important People of the 21st Century.

An inspiration to fans, filmmakers, and entrepreneurs worldwide, Spielberg had no written business plan or college degree when he walked on the Universal Studios lot in the '60s. He merely had a healthy dose of chutzpah (that's Yiddish for balls). Long before he got his break, little Steven was living his passion as a kid — writing stories, making short films, and gaining experience as a novice director ten years before his college summer at the studio. When the opportunity struck, the Universal deal wasn't dumb luck. It was the classic Hollywood tale of passion meets opportunity.

3 Passion Keys to Seize the Day

Key 1) Start and End the Day Motivated
Commit to routines you love at home and work.

Key 2) Surround Yourself with Passionate People
Make a pact with a team or focus friend to inspire each other.

Key 3) Make it Fun!
Games + Smiles + Laughter = Happiness!

Purpose 3
Develop a Healthy
Mind, Body & Soul

"Of course I exercise. I push my luck,
run my mouth, and occasionally jump to conclusions."
ANONYMOUS

Food, Fitness & Brain Formulas

I'M NEITHER A DOCTOR nor a health expert by trade, but throughout my life I played competitive sports, practiced yoga, and studied nutrition. I've noticed however that even the most health-conscious people often neglect the mind-body-soul connection, so this chapter provides a little "success food for thought."

Only you know what's best for your body, especially since everyone has a unique biology and medical history. To all the experts who want to debate the perfect diet, lifestyle, or workout, I bow to your wisdom. In my experience, there's no such thing as a one-size-fits-all formula.

See next page for 6 Rules to
a healthy mind, body & soul ...

Health Rule 1: Maintain a Healthy Mind

A healthy brain routine is essential for memory and cognitive endurance. What we eat, see, hear, touch, or smell affects our ability to think. The good news is anyone can tilt the health formula scale in their favor with a little brain exercise.

My Top 5 Brain Essentials

1 Listen to music or play an instrument.
2 Read or write something new each day.
3 Meditate. A quiet mind is a learning mind.
4 Play memory games like chess, poker, or puzzles.
5 Chat with friends, peers, and strangers about anything new.

Health Rule 2: Develop a Fitness Routine

Physical fitness is critical to longevity (and a healthy brain).
Whether it's sports, yoga, or cross-fitness, get moving daily.
Even with injuries, try to breathe and meditate. It all adds up.

My Top 5 Fitness Essentials

1 Enjoy sports with friends and peers.
2 Go beyond your comfort zone. Try new exercises.
3 Walk or hike outdoors. Fresh air does a body good.
4 Stretch or practice yoga, even just 15-30 minutes per day.
5 Be consistent and find a buddy to join you 3 to 5 days per week.

Health Rule 3: Master Basic Nutrition

Fad diets and fast food are detrimental to long-term health. If you can't pronounce the ingredients, you probably shouldn't eat it!

My Top 5 Nutrition Essentials

1 Drink plenty of water.
2 Eat your fruits and veggies (rich in antioxidants).
3 Learn to balance fats, proteins, fiber, and carbohydrates.
4 Eat smaller portions and healthy snacks for better metabolism.
5 Moderate salt, sugar, dairy, sodas, alcohol, and caffeine in your diet.

138

Health Rule 4: Sleep Well for Total Wellness

Sleep disorders are common and there are many causes. As an athlete, entrepreneur, travel junkie, recovering workaholic, and part-time insomniac, I know first hand that there's a time to chill out or suffer the consequences. Whether you're a rock star, super student, power parent, or midnight manager, listen to your body when it screams for rest. Countless studies show that sleep is one of the most *Essential* rules to a creative mind and productive body.

My Top 5 Sleep Essentials

1 Try to get 6 to 8 hours sleep per night.
2 Avoid sugar and caffeine too close to bedtime.
3 Work and play routines affect sleep, so try to be consistent.
4 Don't sleep with digital gadgets (cell phones keep you wide awake).
5 Avoid bright lights close to bedtime (tablets, computers, television).

Health Rule 5: Reduce the Stress Factor

No matter how resilient you might be, the human body is NOT built for around-the-clock performance. When we constantly push our limits, the mind and body will shut down, often manifesting in disease, panic attacks, or organ failures. If you truly want success, find ways to reduce stress.

Health Rule 6: Unleash Love & Laughter

It's a medical fact that love and laughter are the ultimate cure-all for a common cold or crappy day! Why else would we have a heart and funny bone? So for anyone who wants to be sexier, happier, and much healthier, unleash love and laughter for optimal wellness.

Bonus Rule: Hit the Reset Button

Everyone falls off the health train due to injury, illness, or bad choices. I've been hampered with physical setbacks my whole life (ankle, knee, wrist, shoulder, back, neck). The key is to hit the reset button or ask for help when you feel overwhelmed. Creating better health habits with accountability is critical to your overall well-being.

Purpose 4
Give Back & Make a Difference

> *"You give but little when you give of your possessions.*
> *It is when you give of yourself that you truly give."*
> KAHLIL GIBRAN
> Poet, Artist

> *"I've learned that you shouldn't go through life*
> *with a catcher's mitt on both hands.*
> *You need to be able to throw something back."*
> MAYA ANGELOU
> Poet, Historian, Activist

> *"Long-term profit is not an enduring strategy*
> *if you are not giving back to the communities you serve."*
> HOWARD SCHULTZ
> Founder-CEO, Starbucks

Start Something that Matters

AS I FINISHED WRITING *The 4 Essentials*, I was introduced to social entrepreneur and Founder/Chief Shoe Giver of TOMS Shoes, Blake Mycoskie. Blake's company, and his book, *Start Something that Matters*, had a profound impact on my mission to raise the bar for global education. His story chronicles the giving mission of TOMS and inspires everyone to "start something that matters" in their life, career, or business. With many parallels to *The 4 Essentials*, I wanted to share more of Blake's story for those who may not know how TOMS changed the landscape for social entrepreneurs.

In 2006, Blake befriended children in Argentina and found they had no shoes to protect their feet. Wanting to help, he created TOMS Shoes (short for Tomorrow's Shoes). Blake had no background in shoe design but he understood the principles of companies that do a greater good. He decided he would donate a pair of new shoes to a child in need with each pair of shoes sold by TOMS (one-for-one). When he first returned to Argentina with friends and staff, he delivered 10,000 pairs of shoes to kids in need. He soon learned that walking is the primary mode of transportation in developing countries, but many children in such countries grow up barefoot. These children are at risk when playing, going to school, or walking for miles to seek food, water, or medical help. Shoes prevent their feet from getting sores over those long distances. Without shoes, soil-transmitted parasites can penetrate the skin, cause disease, and even result in amputation. Many times, barefoot children can't attend school because shoes are a required part of their uniform. If they don't receive an education, they don't have the opportunity to realize their potential in life. Simply stated, shoes are a big solution for children worldwide.

When TOMS started in 2006, there weren't many companies talking about social entrepreneurship. By 2016 however, they had delivered over 60 million shoes to kids in need and revolutionized the way consumers think about why they support certain companies. TOMS also expanded their *one-for-one business model* to include the sale of sunglasses, with a portion of profits going to eye surgeries in underdeveloped countries.

Inspired by the one-for-one concept, I launched *The 4 Essentials* and Cliff Michaels Global Learning with a mission to inspire, give back, and raise the bar for education. We start each school with a free audio edition of this book and e-courses for life skills, financial literacy, career strategies, and entrepreneur tools. Since 2012, we've impacted over 50,000 students and professionals, with a goal to impact millions more.

My One-for-One Challenge To You

As Gandhi said, "Be the change you wish to see in the world." Choose your one-for-one. Volunteer time or donate a portion of your income to charity. Sponsor a student, club, or school. Whatever you do, make a difference!

To see how we can help your mission, visit CliffMichaels.com

Purpose 5
Enjoy the Journey

> *"Life moves pretty fast. If you don't stop and look
> around once in a while, you could miss it."*
> MATTHEW BRODERICK
> Ferris Bueller's Day Off (a John Hughes Film)

Always Be Present

OUR PASSION TO ACHIEVE will always demand sacrifice, but no one wants to look back when it's all over and say, "I wish I paid more attention to little things and people who mattered." Since chaos and challenges creep into our lives when least expected, try not to fixate on what's wrong or who to blame. Find magic in the smallest moments and be incredibly present for the big ones. It's far more important to enjoy the journey than obsess about the destination.

Choose your path and breathe it in!

Moments That Matter

- Love
- Play time
- A sunset
- Kind words
- Celebrations
- A brilliant idea
- The punch line
- A kiss
- Friends & family
- The lemonade stand
- The magic & mystery
- The bottom of the ninth
- The book with a torn cover
- The beginning, middle & end

20 Fun Things To Enjoy Your Journey!

1) Rescue a puppy

2) Start a rock n' roll band

3) Gather your gang for movie night

4) Share love and laughter with friends

5) See a concert or dance the night away

6) Invite friends to a fantastic foodie fiesta

7) Give what you can to those less fortunate

8) Hit the town with your favorite teammates

9) Catch a little culture at your local museum

10) Find new ways to celebrate the little things

11) Play, hike, bike, and get sweaty with nature

12) Do something wild you've never done before

13) Start a movement or volunteer for a good cause

14) Go to more carnivals, festivals, and theme parks

15) Pick up the check for a stranger because you can

16) Write your bucket list and commit to the top 3 this year

17) Take a vacation, see the world, and expand your horizons

18) Plan a fun tournament (video, poker, sports, board-games)

19) Start a discussion group with friends who love art and books

20) Play hooky and solemnly swear that you're up to no good !!!

Don't Forget, 80% of Success is Showing Up!

Congratulations!

You've earned a real-world MBA (**M**aster's in **B**asic **A**bilities).
Don't forget to practice and pass it on!

Here's a Recap of Your Top 5 Purpose Principles

1) Ignite Your Personal Power
2) Follow Your Passion
3) Develop a Healthy Mind, Body & Soul
4) Give Back & Make a Difference
5) Enjoy the Journey

FINAL THOUGHTS,

My journey took many roads. Who knew that a failed soccer career would kick me into social entrepreneurship, or that dyslexia would turn me into a writer. For that matter, I never imagined a failed dot-com would teach me the most *Essential* lesson of all — always follow your passion. Coupled with *mindset, strategies, values,* and *purpose,* it all added up to my real-world MBA (a Master's in Basic Abilities).

I learned *The 4 Essentials* from countless mentors who reminded me to keep asking, "WHAT IF?" A lot of thank-you notes and chocolate kisses never hurt. As a final note, the happiest people I know place a premium on fun, friends, family, health, and making a difference. To that end, don't forget to love, laugh, live, and give with passion, humility, and gratitude. When in doubt, chill out, the answers will come.

Here's to your amazing journey!

Cliff Michaels

P.S. Wouldn't it be great if schools and companies joined the education revolution too?

145

The Misfit Hall of Fame

STATISTICALLY, THOSE WHO GRADUATE with a degree are likely to earn more money than those who don't. That said, millions of highly successful people never graduated college due to a personal challenge or preference. So for anyone concerned that a formal degree defines the permanent direction of their life, The Misfit Hall of Fame should dispel all myths.

The following people had no degree when they launched their careers. However, they did earn a real-world MBA (Masters in Basic Abilities).

The Innovators

Misfit's Name	Claim to Fame
Amelia Earhart	Aviation Pioneer
Thomas Edison	Founder, GE and 1,000 patents
Rosa Parks	Civil Rights Activist
Bill Gates	Co-Founder, Microsoft
Jessica Alba	Co Founder, The Honest Company
Steve Jobs	Co-Founder, Apple
Malala Yousafzai	Education Activist, Nobel Prize Winner
Mark Zuckerberg	Founder, Facebook
Ted Turner	Founder, CNN
Richard Branson	Founder, Virgin Group
Coco Chanel	Founder, Chanel Fashion
Anna Wintour	Editor in Chief, Vogue
Michael Dell	Founder, Dell Computers
Hiroshi Yamauchi	President, Nintendo Corporation
Walt Disney	Founder, Disney Films & Disneyland
Mary Kay Ash	Founder, Mary Kay Cosmetics
Milton Hershey	Founder, Hershey's Chocolate
Ralph Lauren	Founder, Ralph Lauren Fashion

The Entertainers

Misfit's Name	Claim to Fame
Adele	Grammy-Winning Singer-Songwriter
Lucille Ball	Emmy-Winning Actor, Comedian
Will Smith	Award-Winning Actor, Producer, Singer
Steven Spielberg	Oscar-Winning Director, Producer
Whoopi Goldberg	Oscar-Winning Actor, Comedian
Woody Allen	Oscar-Winning Actor, Director, Producer
Billie Holiday	Grammy-Winning Singer-Jazz Pioneer
Robert De Niro	Oscar-Winning Actor, Producer
Tom Cruise	Award-Winning Actor, Producer
Dustin Hoffman	Oscar-Winning Actor
Tom Hanks	Oscar-Winning Actor
Matt Damon	Oscar-Winning Screenwriter, Actor
George Clooney	Oscar-Winning Actor, Director
Angelina Jolie	Oscar-Winning Actress
Sean Connery	Oscar Winning Actor
Halle Barry	Oscar-Winning Actor
Charlie Chaplin	Actor, Comedian, Director
Ellen DeGeneres	Actor, Comedian, Talk Show Host
Sammy Davis Jr.	Actor, Comedian, Singer, Dancer
Ray Charles	Grammy-Winning Singer-Songwriter
Steve Martin	Actor, Comedian, Writer, Producer
Carol Burnett	Emmy-Winning Actress, Comedian
Nicole Kidman	Oscar-Winning Actress
Madonna	Grammy Winning Singer, Actor
Jamie Foxx	Oscar-Winning Actor, Comedian, Musician
Rachel Ray	Cook, TV Personality, Best-Selling Author
Michael Caine	Oscar-Winning Actor
Jay-Z	Grammy-Winning Artist, Entrepreneur

The Writers

Misfit's Name	Claim to Fame
Mark Twain	Novelist, Humorist, Entrepreneur
Anne Frank	Diarist, Holocaust Survivor
William Blake	Inspirational Poet & Painter
Maya Angelou	Poet, Historian, Award-Winning Writer
Ray Bradbury	Science Fiction Novelist
Charles Dickens	Novelist & Social Campaigner
William Faulkner	Nobel Prize-Winning Author & Poet
F. Scott Fitzgerald	Novelist & Short Story Writer
Tennessee Williams	Award-Winning Playwright

The Athletes

Misfit's Name	Claim to Fame
Ronda Rousey	12-Time Mixed Martial Arts Champion
Serena Williams	22-Time Grand Slam Champion, Tennis
Venus Williams	7-Time Grand Slam Champion, Tennis
Muhammad Ali	3-Time World Heavyweight Champ, Boxing
Pelé	3-Time World Cup Champion, Soccer
Wayne Gretzky	4-Time Stanley Cup Champion, Hockey
Kobe Bryant	5-Time NBA Champion, Basketball
Roger Federer	17-Time Grand Slam Champion, Tennis
Joe DiMaggio	4-Time World Champion, Baseball
Mario Andretti	4-Time Indy Winner, Auto Racing
Tony Hawk	Pioneering Skateboarder & Entrepreneur
Shaun White	Olympic Gold Medalist, Snowboarding
Wilma Rudolph	3-Time Olympic Gold Medalist, Track & Field
Babe Didrikson Zaharias	10-Time LPGA Major Champion 2-Time Olympic Gold Medalist, Track & Field All-American Basketball Player, Sports Pioneer